HOW TO GET OUT OF BURNOUT IN 2024?

Find your path to healing and rediscover the joy of living

HOW TO GET OUT OF BURNOUT IN 2024?

Find your path to healing and rediscover the joy of living

Vincent Lefebvre

To my son Auguste

PREFACE

As a life coach and mindfulness expert for over two decades, I have had the privilege of supporting thousands of individuals on their path to well-being and fulfillment. Over the years, I have witnessed the evolving trends, challenges and solutions in mental health and wellbeing. It is therefore with great anticipation and deep respect that I approached reading this book.

From the first pages, I was captivated by the depth of the research, the clarity of the ideas and the relevance of the advice offered. This book doesn't just skim the surface of the topics it covers, it delves deep into the roots of the problems we face in our modern society, while offering practical and actionable solutions.

Vincent Lefebvre has weaved together concepts from science, psychology, spirituality and practice to create a comprehensive guide for anyone seeking to heal, grow and thrive in this ever-changing world. The chapters are structured to provide both theoretical understanding and practical tools, making this book both educational and immediately applicable.

What touched me the most was the way he

approached the subject of burnout. Rather than seeing it as a failure or weakness, it is presented as an opportunity for growth, awareness and transformation. This perspective is refreshing and necessary, especially at a time when so many people feel overwhelmed and exhausted.

In conclusion, I heartily recommend this book to anyone looking to deepen their understanding of wellness, overcome personal challenges, or help others on their healing journey. It is a valuable resource that I am confident will have a lasting impact on all who read it.

With all my gratitude for this valuable addition to the wellness literature,

Sophie Smith
Life coach and mindfulness expert.

INTRODUCTION :

Jean Vanier

Overview of burnout and its growing importance in modern society

Burnout. A term that many of us have heard, but few truly understand in all its complexity. It conjures up images of fatigue, exhaustion and a loss of passion for life and work. But what exactly is burnout?

Burnout is a state of emotional, mental and physical exhaustion caused by prolonged stress. It manifests when we feel overwhelmed, emotionally drained and unable to meet the constant demands of our environment. While stress can push us to the limit, making us feel under pressure, burnout is the feeling of being completely drained.

In modern society, the hectic pace of life, combined with the constant pressure to perform, has created fertile ground for burnout. We live in an age where technology allows us to be constantly connected, where the lines between work and personal life are increasingly blurred, and where the quest for perfection is often valued at the expense of our well-being.

The growing importance of burnout in modern society cannot be underestimated. According to various studies, a growing number of people around the world are experiencing the debilitating effects of burnout. It is not just an individual problem, but a societal phenomenon that impacts productivity, mental health and quality of life.

But why is burnout so prevalent today? Several factors contribute to this trend. Globalization, increased competitiveness in the workplace, infobesity and difficulty switching off are all factors that have increased stress levels. Additionally, the stigma associated with seeking help for mental health issues often prevents individuals from seeking the support they need.

In conclusion, burnout is a reflection of the challenges our modern society faces. Recognizing its growing importance is the first step in tackling this problem head on, offering hope and solutions to those who suffer from it. In the following chapters, we will explore in depth the causes, symptoms and, above all, ways to overcome and prevent this modern scourge.

Purpose of the book
and who it is for

The main objective of this book is twofold. Firstly, it aims to raise awareness among the general public of the reality of burnout, by demystifying preconceived ideas and highlighting the real causes, symptoms and consequences of this state of exhaustion. Second, it aspires to provide concrete tools, strategies and resources to help those affected by burnout, directly or indirectly, find paths to healing and prevention.

This book is aimed at a wide range of readers:

1. **For Individuals Experiencing Burnout** : For those experiencing the overwhelming effects of burnout, this book offers an in-depth understanding of what they are going through, as well as practical steps to regain balance and well-being.

2. **For Loved Ones** : For friends, partners and family members who are watching their loved ones struggle with burnout, this guide offers insights to understand and effectively support their loved ones.

3. **For Professionals** : Managers, business leaders and human resources professionals will find valuable information on how to recognize

the signs of burnout within their teams and what steps they can take to create a healthy work environment .

4. **To Therapists and Counselors** : This book can serve as a complementary resource for mental health professionals who seek to deepen their understanding of burnout and equip their patients with the tools necessary to overcome this condition.

5. **For the Curious and Seeking** : For those interested in psychology, mental health or contemporary societal challenges, this book offers an in-depth exploration of a phenomenon that is increasingly prevalent in our modern society.

In short, this book is an invitation to reflection, understanding and action. It aims to equip every reader with the knowledge and skills needed to deal with burnout, whether for themselves, for a loved one or for society as a whole.

CHAPTER 1: UNDERSTANDIN G BURNOUT

"Burnout is the result of an imbalance between who we are and who we think we should be."

Arianna Huffington

1.1 "Causes and symptoms of burnout":

1.1.1 Origins of Burnout

Burnout, although widely recognized in today's society, is not a new phenomenon. Its origins can be traced through history, although the term itself and formal recognition of its impact on mental health are relatively recent.

Antiquity and Middle Ages:
Even if the term "burnout" did not exist, ancient

texts refer to states of emotional and physical exhaustion. Greek philosophers, for example, spoke of acedia, a state of torpor and apathy. Christian monks of the Middle Ages also described a similar state, often linked to the isolation and monotony of monastic life.

Industrial Revolution :

With the advent of the Industrial Revolution, workers were subjected to harsh and often inhumane working conditions. The long hours, lack of workers' rights, and unsafe conditions led to physical and emotional exhaustion, although it has not yet been termed "burnout."

20th Century :

It was in the 1970s that the term "burnout" was first introduced to describe professional exhaustion. Dr. Herbert Freudenberger, a clinical psychologist, used the term to describe the symptoms of burnout he observed in healthcare professionals. He defined burnout as an "erosion of values, dignity, spirit and will" resulting from occupational stress.

Modern Factors :

Today, burnout is recognized as being influenced by a combination of individual, interpersonal and organizational factors. Rapidly changing technology, globalization, infobesity and the constant pressure to be "connected" have all contributed to the increase in cases of burnout.

In conclusion, although the concept of burnout as we know it today is relatively new, emotional and physical exhaustion is a challenge that humanity has faced for centuries. Understanding its historical and cultural origins can help us better understand the complexity of this phenomenon and develop more effective strategies to prevent and treat it.

1.1.2 Professional Causes

Burnout is often associated with professional factors. Although it can occur in any life context, the workplace is a breeding ground for conditions that lead to emotional, mental and physical exhaustion. Here are some of the main professional causes of burnout:

1. Work Overload :
One of the most common causes of burnout is work overload. Regular overtime, unrealistic expectations and a constant workload without sufficient rest time can quickly lead to burnout.

2. Lack of Control :
Feeling powerless or unable to influence decisions that affect your work can lead to a feeling of loss of control. This may relate to schedules, assigned projects or working methods.

3. Inadequate Compensation and Recognition :
Not feeling valued or rewarded for your work can lead to feelings of frustration and demotivation. This may be linked to insufficient remuneration, a lack of recognition or a lack of prospects for professional development.

4. Dysfunctional Group Dynamics :

Working in an environment where there is conflict, distrust or a lack of support from colleagues or superiors can contribute to burnout.

5. Work-Life Imbalance :

The inability to establish a clear separation between work and personal life, especially with the rise of teleworking, can lead to a feeling of always being "on duty", which can lead to to exhaustion.

6. Values in Conflict :

When there is a mismatch between an individual's personal values and the values of the organization they work for, it can lead to a feeling of disenchantment or disillusionment.

7. Lack of Role Clarity :

Not having a clear understanding of one's responsibilities or being assigned conflicting tasks can lead to confusion and frustration.

8. Job Insecurity :

The constant fear of losing your job, especially in an unstable economic climate, can be a major source of stress and anxiety.

9. Emotional Demands :

Certain professions, such as those in the health or social services sector, require intense emotional involvement, which can increase the risk of burnout.

In short, professional burnout is the result of a combination of factors related to the work environment, professional expectations and interpersonal dynamics. Recognizing and addressing these causes is essential to preventing burnout and promoting a healthy work environment.

1.1.3 Personal Causes

While burnout is often associated with professional factors, it is essential to recognize that personal elements can also contribute to this state of exhaustion. These personal causes, often rooted in the psychology and lifestyle habits of the individual, can act as catalysts or amplifiers of burnout. Here are some of the main personal causes:

1. Perfectionism :
Individuals who tend toward perfectionism may set unrealistic standards for themselves and put themselves under constant pressure to achieve excellence. This incessant quest for perfection can lead to frustration and burnout.

2. Difficulty Saying No :
People who have difficulty setting boundaries or refusing additional requests may find themselves overwhelmed by excessive commitments and responsibilities.

3. Low Self-Esteem :
Having low self-esteem can make someone more vulnerable to burnout. These individuals may feel the constant need to prove their worth, which can lead to burnout.

4. Tendency to Self-Neglect :
Neglecting one's own needs, whether in terms of

sleep, eating or leisure, can accelerate the onset of burnout.

5. Lack of Stress Management Skills :
Not having the tools or techniques to effectively manage stress can make a person more susceptible to burnout.

6. History of Mental Health Conditions :
Individuals with a history of depression, anxiety or other mental health conditions may be more vulnerable to burnout.

7. Tendency to Isolate :
Isolating yourself from others, whether by avoiding social interactions or not sharing your feelings, can worsen feelings of loneliness and exhaustion.

8. Unrealistic Expectations :
Setting unachievable goals or expecting too much of yourself without considering your own limits can lead to disappointment and burnout.

9. Relationship Difficulties :
Conflict or tension in personal relationships, whether with partners, family or friends, can contribute to stress and burnout.

In conclusion, burnout is not only the result of external or professional factors. Personality traits, lifestyle habits, and personal experiences play a crucial role in an individual's susceptibility to burnout. Recognizing and addressing these personal causes is just as essential as addressing professional factors for complete recovery and effective prevention of burnout.

1.1.4 Physical Symptoms

Burnout, although often associated with emotional and mental symptoms, also presents a range of physical manifestations. These symptoms can vary in intensity and frequency, but they are often a reflection of the chronic stress and exhaustion that those affected feel. Here are some of the most common physical symptoms associated with burnout:

1. Chronic Fatigue :
One of the most common signs of burnout is persistent fatigue. Affected people may feel constantly exhausted, even after a good night's sleep.

2. Sleep Disorders :
Insomnia, frequent awakenings during the night or waking up early in the morning without being able to go back to sleep are common among people experiencing burnout.

3. Headaches :
Frequent or persistent headaches can be a sign of tension or stress.

4. Muscle Pain and Tension :
Neck, shoulder or back pain is common, often due to chronic muscle tension.

5. Digestive Disorders :
Stress and exhaustion can affect the digestive system, leading to symptoms such as nausea, abdominal pain, diarrhea or constipation.

6. Heart Palpitations :

Some people may experience palpitations or an irregular heartbeat, often related to anxiety or stress.

7. Lowered Immunity :

Burnout can weaken the immune system, making individuals more susceptible to infections, such as colds or the flu.

8. Changes in Appetite :

This can manifest itself as a loss of appetite or, conversely, overeating.

9. Dizziness or Lightheadedness :

In some cases, people may feel dizzy or feel like the room is spinning.

10. Weight Changes :

Whether weight gain or loss, unexplained changes can be a sign of an imbalance due to stress or exhaustion.

It is crucial to recognize that these physical symptoms are not only the result of work-related stress, but may also be a reflection of other medical conditions. Therefore, anyone experiencing these symptoms should consult a healthcare professional for a proper diagnosis. Recognizing and treating the physical manifestations of burnout is an essential step toward healing and well-being.

1.1.5 Emotional Symptoms

The emotional symptoms of burnout are often the first to be noticed because they directly influence how a person interacts with their environment and others. These emotional displays may be subtle at first, but they usually intensify as burnout progresses. Here are some of the most common emotional symptoms associated with burnout:

1. Feeling of Exhaustion :

Beyond simple fatigue, it is a feeling of total exhaustion that encompasses both body and mind. Daily tasks can seem insurmountable.

2. Cynicism and Detachment :

People experiencing burnout can become cynical about their work, their colleagues or even their life in general. They may also feel detached or disinterested in their responsibilities.

3. Feeling of Ineffectiveness :

A persistent feeling of not accomplishing much or of not being up to the task, even if this is not the case in reality.

4. Irritability :

Low tolerance for frustration, leading to mood swings or overreactions to small problems.

5. Anxiety :

Constant feelings of worry or nervousness, often accompanied by physical symptoms such as palpitations or sweating.

6. Depression :

Feelings of sadness, hopelessness, or emptiness, which may be accompanied by a loss of interest in usual activities or an inability to feel pleasure.

7. Feelings of Isolation :

A feeling of loneliness or disconnection from

others, even in the presence of colleagues, friends or family.

8. Loss of Motivation :

A lack of enthusiasm or interest in work or other activities, even those that were previously sources of pleasure.

9. Feeling of Injustice :

A feeling that one is mistreated, underestimated, or not recognized for one's efforts.

10. Self-Doubt :

A decline in self-confidence, accompanied by constant questions about one's worth or skills.

It is essential to understand that these emotional symptoms are not a weakness or character flaw. They are the result of chronic stress and emotional overload. Recognizing these signs and seeking help is crucial for healing and preventing further deterioration in mental and emotional health.

1.1.6 Behavioral Symptoms

Behavioral symptoms of burnout are outward manifestations that reflect the emotional and physical turmoil a person feels. These symptoms can affect not only the person themselves, but also those around them professionally and personally. Here are some of the behavioral symptoms commonly associated with burnout:

1. Social Withdrawal :

People experiencing burnout may withdraw from colleagues, friends and family, avoiding social interactions and preferring isolation.

2. Procrastination :
A constant postponement of tasks, especially those that were previously accomplished with ease.

3. Absenteeism at Work :
An increase in days of absence, frequent lateness or even the desire to quit your job.

4. Negligence of Responsibilities :
A lack of attention or care in carrying out tasks, whether professional or personal.

5. Excessive Substance Use :
An increase in the consumption of alcohol, caffeine, tobacco or even medications, in an attempt to manage stress or escape.

6. Changes in Appetite :
This can result in episodes of overeating or, conversely, in a loss of appetite.

7. Increased Irritability :
Excessive reactions to minor annoyances, frequent conflicts with colleagues or family.

8. Neglect of Personal Hygiene :
A lack of attention to personal appearance, such as not showering regularly or being careless about one's clothing.

9. Making Hasty Decisions :
Impulsive or poorly thought out decisions, often regrettable later.

10. Avoidance of New Tasks :
A reluctance to take on new responsibilities or take on new projects.

These behavioral symptoms are often the visible

warning signs of burnout. They can have detrimental consequences on a person's career, relationships, and overall health. It is therefore crucial to recognize them early and take steps to treat the underlying cause and mitigate these behaviors.

1.1.7 Consequences on Mental Health

Burnout, although initially perceived as a strictly professional phenomenon, has profound repercussions on a person's mental health. The consequences can be both immediate and long-term, affecting quality of life, relationships and the ability to function on a daily basis. Here are some of the major consequences of burnout on mental health:

1. Depression :

Burnout can lead to depressive episodes, characterized by persistent sadness, loss of interest in usual activities, feelings of hopelessness and, in severe cases, suicidal thoughts.

2. Anxiety :

People experiencing burnout can develop anxiety disorders, ranging from generalized anxiety to panic attacks, often triggered by situations that were not previously stressful.

3. Attention Disorder :

The ability to concentrate, pay attention to details or complete tasks can be seriously affected, leading to errors or reduced productivity.

4. Reduced Self-Esteem :
A constant feeling of failure or inadequacy can erode self-confidence, leading to doubts about one's skills and worth.

5. Insomnia :
Sleep problems, whether it's difficulty falling asleep, waking up at night or waking up early, can worsen exhaustion and affect mental health.

6. Feelings of Alienation :
A feeling of disconnection or distance from others, combined with a feeling of isolation, can reinforce feelings of loneliness and incomprehension.

7. Mild Paranoia :
In some cases, burnout can lead to increased distrust of colleagues or hierarchy, perceived as threats or sources of stress.

8. Irritability and Agitation :
Exacerbated emotional reactions, low tolerance for frustration, and a tendency toward agitation may become common.

9. Apathy :
A lack of interest or enthusiasm for daily tasks, a feeling of emptiness or indifference to events.

10. Psychosomatic Disorders :
Physical symptoms without an apparent medical cause, such as pain, headaches or digestive disturbances, may reflect underlying mental disorders.

It is essential to understand that burnout is not simply a temporary state of fatigue. It's a warning sign that something is wrong with the way a person handles the stress and demands of their life. Recognizing these mental health consequences and seeking help is crucial for recovery and preventing further deterioration.

1.2 Statistics and facts about burnout around the world

1.2.1 Global Recognition of Burnout

The global recognition of burnout as a serious and worrying phenomenon has undergone significant evolution over the last decades. Here is an overview of this recognition and its impact on public health and the professional world:

1. Classification by WHO :

In 2019, the World Health Organization (WHO) officially recognized burnout as a "work-related phenomenon" in its International Classification of Diseases (ICD-11). Although not classified as a medical illness, this recognition has highlighted the importance of treating burnout as a serious workplace health problem.

2. Growing Prevalence :

Studies in various countries have shown a steady increase in the number of people reporting symptoms of burnout, particularly among high-demand occupations, such as healthcare, teaching, and emergency services. .

3. Economic Impact :

Burnout is costly to economies around the

world. Associated costs include lost productivity, absenteeism, employee turnover and healthcare costs. Some estimates suggest that the cost of burnout to the global economy is in the billions.

4. Legal Recognition :

In some countries, burnout is recognized as an occupational illness, which allows workers to benefit from specific compensation or protections. This legal recognition highlights the need for employers to take steps to prevent and treat burnout.

5. Awareness Initiatives :

Faced with the rise in burnout, many organizations, both governmental and non-governmental, have launched awareness campaigns to educate the public and employers about the causes, symptoms and means of preventing burnout.

6. Research and Studies :

The global recognition of burnout has led to an increase in research and studies on the subject. These studies aim to better understand the underlying mechanisms, the populations most at risk and the most effective interventions.

7. Corporate Initiatives :

Many companies across the world have started to recognize the importance of the mental health of their employees. Wellness programs, stress management training, and flexible work policies have become common in many organizations.

In conclusion, the global recognition of burnout

reflects a growing awareness of the importance of mental health at work. As the world continues to adapt to ever-changing ways of working, the need to address and prevent burnout will remain a major priority for policymakers, employers and healthcare professionals.

1.2.2 Prevalence of Burnout

Burnout prevalence refers to the proportion of people within a given population who have experienced or are currently experiencing symptoms of burnout. Understanding prevalence is essential to measure the scale of the problem and to guide interventions and policies. Here's a look at the prevalence of burnout around the world:

1. Global Trends :

According to various studies and surveys, between 10% and 30% of workers worldwide report having experienced symptoms of burnout at some point in their career. These figures may vary depending on countries, sectors and professions.

2. High-Risk Professions :

Some professions are particularly vulnerable to burnout due to the demanding nature of their work. Healthcare professionals, teachers, social workers, police officers and firefighters are among the most affected groups.

3. Impact of Technology :

With the advent of modern communication technologies, many people feel "always connected", which can lead to increased stress and burnout. Around 40% of office workers say they feel constant pressure to be available outside of work hours.

4. Youth Burnout :

Younger workers, particularly millennials and Gen Z, report higher levels of burnout compared to previous generations. Reasons may include high job expectations, student debt, and increased competition in the job market.

5. Burnout and Gender :

Although burnout affects both men and women, some studies suggest that women may be slightly more likely to experience burnout symptoms, particularly due to dual workloads and family responsibilities.

6. Regional Variations :

The prevalence of burnout can vary significantly from region to region. For example, countries with an intensive work culture, such as Japan or South Korea, may have higher rates of burnout compared to countries with better work-life balance.

7. Evolution over Time :

Over the decades, the prevalence of burnout has increased, reflecting changes in work styles, professional expectations and societal challenges. In short, the prevalence of burnout is a key indicator of the mental health of workers around the world. Recognizing the scale of the problem is the first step to putting in place preventive measures and targeted interventions to support those affected.

1.2.3 Demographic Impact

The demographic impact of burnout refers to how different age groups, genders, ethnicities, and other demographics are affected by burnout. Understanding these variations is crucial for targeting interventions and prevention measures. Here is an overview of the demographic impact of burnout:

1. Age :

· **Young Adults** : Younger workers, particularly those in Generations Y and Z, report higher levels of burnout. Challenges such as entering the job market, high expectations and economic uncertainties can contribute to this phenomenon.

· **Middle-Aged Adults** : This group, often sandwiched between work and family responsibilities, may also experience high levels of burnout, particularly due to pressure to balance work and home life.

· **Seniors** : Although less common, burnout can also affect older workers, particularly those facing challenges such as impending retirement or feeling not up to date with modern technologies.

2. Gender :

· **Women** : Studies show that women may be slightly more likely to experience symptoms of burnout. This may be due to factors such as double workload, family responsibilities and specific work challenges.

·   **Men** : Although men are also affected, they may express their burnout in different ways, often by masking their feelings or avoiding seeking help.

3. Ethnic and Cultural Background :

Different cultures have varied attitudes towards work, rest and mental health. In some cultures, burnout may be less recognized or stigmatized, which may affect reported prevalence and help-seeking.

4. Professional Sector :

Certain sectors, such as healthcare, education and emergency services, have higher burnout rates due to the stressful and demanding nature of their work.

5. Education Level :

People with higher levels of education may feel different pressures, such as high performance expectations, which can contribute to burnout.

6. Socio-economic situation :

People in precarious economic situations or facing financial challenges may be more likely to experience stress and burnout due to economic pressures.

7. Family Situation :

People with family responsibilities, such as single parents or those caring for elderly or ill family members, may be particularly vulnerable to burnout.

In conclusion, the demographic impact of burnout shows that although this phenomenon can affect everyone, certain groups may be more at risk due to specific factors. A nuanced understanding of these variations is essential for developing targeted and effective interventions.

1.2.4 Economic Consequences

Burnout, although initially perceived as an individual problem, has major economic repercussions that extend well beyond the affected individual. The economic consequences of burnout affect businesses, healthcare systems and the economy as a whole. Here is an overview of the economic implications of burnout:

1. Absenteeism :

One of the most immediate effects of burnout is increased absenteeism from work. Exhausted employees are more likely to take sick days, leading to lost productivity for the company and additional costs in replacement or job coverage.

2. High Turnover :

Employees suffering from burnout are more likely to leave their jobs, leading to recruiting, training and onboarding costs for companies. Staff turnover can also affect the morale of other employees and disrupt work continuity.

3. Decreased Productivity :

Even when employees are present at work, burnout can lead to decreased productivity, as those affected may have difficulty concentrating, making decisions or being creative.

4. Medical Costs :

People suffering from burnout are more likely to develop health problems, ranging from sleep disorders to cardiovascular disease. This leads to increased medical costs for employers and health systems.

5. Errors and Accidents :

In professions where precision and attention are crucial, such as medicine or driving, burnout can increase the risk of errors or accidents, with potentially serious and costly consequences.

6. Effects on Economic Growth :

On a macroeconomic scale, an exhausted workforce can hamper economic growth. Businesses may struggle to innovate, grow or respond to market needs, which can impact national competitiveness.

7. Social Costs :

Beyond direct economic costs, burnout can result in social costs, such as increased divorce rates, family problems, or mental health problems in the community.

8. Investing in Wellbeing :

Recognizing the high costs of burnout, many companies are now actively investing in wellness and mental health programs for their employees. Although this represents an upfront cost, the investment can provide a significant return on investment in terms of reduced absenteeism, employee turnover and medical costs.

In short, the economic consequences of burnout are broad and affect many aspects of the economy. Recognizing and addressing burnout not only as an individual health problem, but also as an economic issue, is essential for policymakers, employers and society as a whole.

1.2.5 Regional Risk Factors

Risk factors for burnout can vary significantly across regions of the world, due to cultural, economic and social differences. Each region has its own challenges and dynamics that can influence the prevalence and nature of burnout. Here is an overview of regional risk factors associated with burnout:

1. North America :

· **Intense work culture** : Valuing long work hours and constant availability, especially in cities like New York or Los Angeles, can increase the risk of burnout.

· **Professional competition** : The pressure to stand out and succeed in competitive industries can lead to increased stress.

2. Europe :

· **Work-life balance** : Although many European countries value work-life balance, sectors such as finance in London or startups in Berlin can pose high risks of burnout.

· **Societal expectations** : In some cultures, there can be a lot of pressure to succeed academically and professionally, which can contribute to burnout.

3. Asia :

· **Culture of overwork** : In countries like Japan and South Korea, overwork is a recognized problem, with specific terms like "karoshi" or "death from overwork."

· **Academic Pressure** : In many Asian countries, there is a lot of pressure on young people to succeed academically, which can establish patterns of stress and burnout from a young age.

4. Latin America :

· **Economic instability** : In some areas, economic instability and professional challenges can increase stress and the risk of burnout.

· **Cultural norms** : Valuing family and relationships can sometimes conflict with work demands, creating tension.

5. Africa :

· **Socio-economic challenges** : In many parts of Africa, challenges such as poverty, conflict and disease can increase overall stress, contributing to burnout.

· **Limited access to mental health care** : In many areas, there may be a lack of access to appropriate mental health resources, exacerbating the effects of burnout.

6. Oceania :

· **Geographic isolation** : In countries like Australia and New Zealand, geographic distance can sometimes contribute to a feeling of isolation or disconnection.

· **Sector pressures** : Sectors such as mining in Australia may present specific risks of burnout due to the nature of the work.

In conclusion, although burnout is a global phenomenon, the risk factors and manifestations can vary considerably from one region to another. A nuanced understanding of these regional factors is essential for developing effective interventions and prevention strategies.

1.2.6 Effects on Overall Health

Burnout, although often associated with professional consequences, has profound repercussions on the overall health of individuals. These effects are not just limited to mental health, but also extend to physical health, with potentially long-lasting consequences. Here is an overview of the effects of burnout on overall health:

1. Mental Disorders :

· **Depression** : Burnout is closely linked to depression, with symptoms such as sadness, loss of interest and hopelessness.

· **Anxiety** : People suffering from burnout may also experience high levels of anxiety, resulting in constant worry, restlessness, and increased tension.

2. Physical Problems :

· **Sleep problems** : Insomnia or sleep disturbances are common among people suffering from burnout.

· **Aches and pains** : Headaches, muscle aches or back pain may occur.

· **Digestive problems** : Burnout can lead to problems such as nausea, abdominal pain or digestive problems.

3. **Chronic Diseases** :

· **Cardiovascular disease** : Chronic stress associated with burnout can increase the risk of heart disease.

· **Diabetes** : Stress can affect blood sugar regulation, potentially increasing the risk of type 2 diabetes.

4. **Immune System** :

· **Vulnerability to infections** : A weakened immune system can make a person more susceptible to common infections like colds or flu.

· **Delayed Healing** : Chronic stress can slow down the body's healing process.

5. **Behavioral Effects** :

· **Increased alcohol or drug use** : Some people may turn to alcohol or drugs as a means of self-medication.

· **Social withdrawal** : People suffering from burnout may isolate themselves from family, friends or co-workers.

6. **Cognitive Effects** :

· **Difficulty concentrating** : Burnout can make it difficult to concentrate or complete simple tasks.

· **Memory loss** : Frequent forgetting or difficulty remembering information may occur.

7. Repercussions on Longevity :

· **Increased mortality** : In extreme cases, chronic stress and its associated effects can reduce longevity.

In short, burnout is much more than simple professional fatigue. Its effects on overall health are broad and can have long-lasting consequences if left untreated. It is therefore essential to recognize the signs of burnout and take steps to support recovery and well-being.

1.2.7 Global Responses and Initiatives

Faced with the alarming increase in cases of burnout around the world, various organizations, governments and institutions have taken steps to recognize, prevent and treat this phenomenon. Here is an overview of global responses and initiatives to burnout:

1. Recognition by WHO :

· In 2019, the World Health Organization (WHO) officially recognized burnout as a "work-related phenomenon" in the 11th Revision of the International Classification of Diseases (ICD-11). This recognition has highlighted the importance of treating burnout as a serious health problem.

2. Flexible Work Policies :

· Many countries and companies have begun to adopt flexible work policies, allowing employees to work from home or adjust their schedules to better balance work and home life.

3. Awareness Programs :

·   Awareness campaigns have been launched in several countries to educate the public about the signs, causes and consequences of burnout. These campaigns also aim to destigmatize help-seeking.

4. Workplace Well-being Initiatives :

·   Companies around the world have started implementing wellness programs for their employees, offering resources such as meditation sessions, fitness classes, and stress management workshops.

5. Legislation on Working Hours :

·   Some countries, such as France, have passed laws limiting working hours and guaranteeing the right to disconnect, allowing employees to disconnect from work during their off hours.

6. Training of Managers :

·   Recognizing that management style can contribute to burnout, many companies now offer training to managers to help them recognize the signs of burnout in their subordinates and provide appropriate support.

7. Technological Initiatives :

·   With the advent of technology, apps and platforms have been developed to help individuals manage stress, practice mindfulness, and improve their overall well-being.

8. Forums and Conferences :

·   Forums and conferences are regularly held globally to discuss best practices, research and innovations in burnout prevention and treatment.

9. Community Support :

·   Support groups and online communities have sprung up, providing a space for people affected by burnout to share their experiences and find support.

In conclusion, the growing recognition of burnout as a global problem has led to a multitude of initiatives aimed at combating it. Although much remains to be done, these collective efforts show awareness and a desire to tackle this problem head on.

CHAPTER 2: PERSONAL TESTIMONIES

"Burnout is a sign that we have been left to our own devices for too long."

Rob Bell

2.1 Stories of people who have experienced and overcome burnout

2.1.1 The senior manager

Marc, 45, was the CEO of a growing technology company. With a team of over 500 people under his leadership and investors constantly chasing him for results, the pressure was immense. Every day, he got up before dawn, checked his emails before even getting out of bed, and spent long hours at the office, often until late at night.

At first, Marc saw this routine as the price to pay for success. He was proud of his dedication and his ability to handle such pressure. However, over time, signs of fatigue began to appear. He was constantly exhausted, irritable and had difficulty concentrating. Weekends, which were once dedicated to relaxing with family, were now taken over by work.

One morning, Marc collapsed in his office. He was rushed to hospital where the diagnosis was made: severe burnout. Doctors advised him to take extended leave and reconsider his lifestyle.

After several months of rest, therapy and reflection, Marc realized that his identity and worth should not be defined solely by his work. He started delegating more, setting clear work-life boundaries, and prioritizing his mental and physical health.

With the support of his family, a life coach and a therapist, Marc managed to overcome his burnout. He returned to his role as CEO, but with a new perspective and strategies for managing stress. He also implemented wellness programs within his company to help his employees avoid burnout.

Marc's story is a powerful reminder that no one is safe from burnout, regardless of their position or status. She also highlights the importance of recognizing the warning signs and taking steps to protect your mental and physical health.

2.1.2 The Nurse on the Front Line

Sophie, 32, was a dedicated nurse working in a big city hospital. Every day she witnessed the challenges, pains and miracles of life. She loved her work deeply, finding deep meaning in helping others in their most vulnerable moments.

When the global pandemic hit in 2020, Sophie's workload increased exponentially. Overtime became the norm, and every day she faced a sea of patients, the fear of contagion, and the pain of losing patients despite all efforts.

As the months passed, the emotional weight of the situation began to weigh heavily on Sophie. She felt constantly exhausted, often cried after her shifts, and had trouble sleeping. She felt guilty for not doing enough for her patients and feared she wasn't good enough.

One evening, after a particularly grueling shift, Sophie collapsed in tears in the hospital changing rooms. She realized she was on the verge of burnout. She made the difficult decision to request time off to focus on her own mental health.

While on leave, Sophie sought support from a trauma therapist. She also joined a support group for healthcare professionals, where she was able to share her experiences and find comfort from colleagues facing similar challenges.

Over time, Sophie learned to recognize the importance of taking care of herself so that she could take care of others. She has developed strategies to manage stress, such as meditation, journaling and regular mindfulness practice.

When she returned to the hospital, Sophie was a transformed nurse. She continued to serve her patients with compassion, but with a new awareness of her own limitations and needs.

Sophie's story highlights the unique challenges healthcare professionals face, particularly in crisis situations. She also reiterates the importance of self-compassion and seeking support when facing intense emotional challenges.

2.1.3 The Start-up Entrepreneur

Thomas, 28, was the archetype of the modern entrepreneur. After graduating from a prestigious business school, he launched his own technology start-up with the ambition of revolutionizing the finance industry. With a brilliant idea, a solid initial investment and a passionate team, everything seemed aligned for success.

The first months were electrifying. Thomas worked day and night, driven by the passion for his project and the vision of his company becoming a major player in the market. Each awakening was an opportunity, each bedtime a reflection on the challenges of the next day.

However, over time, the challenges have multiplied. Competition was fierce, investor expectations were high, and the pressure to constantly be innovative and growing was overwhelming. Thomas began sacrificing his sleep, his social life and even his health for his start-up.

One day, after a series of disappointments, including the loss of a major client and internal disagreements within the team, Thomas felt completely overwhelmed. He realized he could no longer distinguish his own identity from that of his company. The line between his personal and professional life had blurred, and he felt trapped in his own creation.

It was at that moment that Thomas realized that he was in full burnout. He decided to take a step back, temporarily step away from his business and seek help. With the support of a professional coach and therapist, Thomas learned to reprioritize, set healthy boundaries, and delegate more.

When he returned to his start-up, it was with a renewed perspective. He has put structures in place to ensure a better work-life balance for himself and his team. He also learned the importance of resilience, adaptability and stepping back from challenges.

Thomas' story illustrates the unique challenges entrepreneurs face, especially in the fast-paced world of start-ups. She highlights the importance of taking care of yourself, even (and especially) when running a business.

2.1.4 The Creative Artist

Élise, 35, was a talented artist, known for her vibrant paintings and immersive installations.

From a young age, she always knew she was destined to create. Each brushstroke, each color choice was an extension of his soul, a way of expressing his deepest emotions and connecting with the world around him.

Over the years, Élise has acquired a certain notoriety in the art world. His exhibitions were eagerly awaited and his works sold for ever higher prices. However, with recognition came increasing pressure to constantly produce, to meet audience expectations and to constantly reinvent oneself.

Creativity, once fluid and natural for Élise, has become a struggle. She often found herself facing a blank canvas, paralyzed by the anxiety of the blank page. Deadlines were getting closer, the criticism was sometimes harsh, and Élise was beginning to doubt her talent and her place in the art world.

One evening, after tearing up a painting she had worked on for weeks, Élise realized she was burning out. The passion and joy she once felt while creating had been overshadowed by stress, pressure, and doubt.

She decided to take a break from the art scene and retreated to a small house by the sea. There, far from the spotlight and expectations, Élise rediscovered her love for art. She began painting for herself, experimenting with new techniques and reconnecting with her inner creativity.

Over time, Élise returned to the artistic scene, but with a new perspective. She learned to set boundaries, say no when necessary, and prioritize her mental and emotional well-being.

Élise's story reminds us that creativity cannot be forced and that artists, like everyone else, are vulnerable to burnout. She highlights the importance of staying true to yourself, taking a step back when necessary, and remembering why you started creating in the first place.

2.1.5 The Dedicated Educator

Marc, 42, was a passionate teacher, dedicated to educating his students and creating a positive learning environment. For more than two decades, he taught history at a suburban high school, inspiring generations of students with his enthusiasm and in-depth knowledge of the subject.

Each year, Marc went above and beyond his duties, leading field trips, tutoring struggling students after class, and even starting history clubs to encourage a passion for the subject outside of the classroom. For him, teaching was not just a job, it was a vocation.

However, with time, the educational landscape began to change. Budgets were being cut, classes were getting bigger, and the pressure to perform well on exams was increasing. Marc often found himself juggling the needs of his students, administrative expectations, and the daily challenges of the classroom.

Fatigue insidiously set in. The long hours, weekends spent preparing for lessons, and constant stress began to take a toll on Marc. He felt exhausted, irritable and less passionate about his work.

One day, after an altercation with a colleague over a minor subject, Marc collapsed in tears in the teachers' lounge. He realized he was burning out, emotionally and physically exhausted by the incessant demands of his job.

Marc made the decision to take a sabbatical. During this time, he traveled, reconnected with his passion for history by visiting historical sites, and sought the support of a therapist to treat his burnout.

Upon his return, Marc adopted a more balanced approach to teaching. He learned to delegate, set boundaries and take time for himself. He also advocated for better working conditions for teachers, recognizing that educator well-being is essential to student success.

Marc's story highlights the challenges educators face in the modern world. It reminds us of the importance of taking care of ourselves, even in a profession as altruistic as teaching, and highlights the crucial role that teachers play in training future generations.

2.1.6 The Stay-at-Home Parent

Sophie, 38, had always dreamed of being a mother. When she gave birth to her twins, she made the decision to leave her position as marketing director to devote herself fully to raising her children. The first years were filled with simple joys: the first steps, laughter, games and daily discoveries.

But as children grew older, the challenges of parenting became more complex. Between school activities, medical appointments, running the household and the emotional needs of two growing children, Sophie constantly felt overwhelmed. Without the structure and recognition her job provided, she began to feel a sense of isolation and inadequacy.

The days blended together, and Sophie often found herself juggling several tasks at once, never really taking time for herself. The pressure of society, which often romanticizes motherhood and downplays the challenges of being a stay-at-home parent, added to her feelings of guilt and inadequacy.

One morning, after a sleepless night of consoling one sick child and dealing with another's crisis, Sophie broke down in tears, realizing that she was exhausted, not only physically, but also emotionally. She understood that she was burned out.

With the support of her partner, Sophie sought help. She joined a parent support group, where she was able to share her challenges and feelings with others in the same situation. She also began to take time for herself, whether it was to exercise, read or simply rest.

Sophie also realized the importance of asking for

help and delegating certain tasks. She began to share parental responsibilities more equally with her partner and to seek help from family and friends when necessary.

Sophie's story highlights the often underestimated challenges that stay-at-home parents face. She reminds us that self-care is essential, even in a role as dedicated as parenting, and that asking for help is not a sign of weakness, but of strength.

2.1.7 The Young Professional

Lucas, 26, was the epitome of ambition. Freshly graduated from a major business school, he landed a position in a prestigious consulting company in Paris. For him, it was the start of a promising career, filled with opportunities and success.

Upon his arrival, Lucas immersed himself in his work with unprecedented ardor. He was often the first to arrive at the office and the last to leave, sacrificing his weekends and evenings to meet the expectations of his superiors and stand out from his colleagues. Every project was an opportunity to prove his worth, and Lucas would stop at nothing to impress.

But behind this facade of success and determination, Lucas was beginning to feel the effects of this constant pressure. Sleepless nights, the stress of deadlines and fierce competition with colleagues began to take a toll on his mental and physical health. Moments of relaxation were rare, and Lucas felt constantly on edge, afraid of making a mistake or not being good enough.

One evening, after a particularly tense meeting with a client, Lucas felt intense pain in his chest. Thinking he was having a heart attack, he rushed to the hospital, only to discover it was actually a panic attack.

This was the trigger for Lucas. He realized that his relentless quest for perfection and recognition had led him to the brink. He was burned out.

With the support of his family and friends, Lucas began a journey of recovery. He saw a therapist to treat his anxiety and learned to set boundaries in his professional life. He also realized the importance of work-life balance and began prioritizing his health and well-being.

Lucas' story is a powerful reminder of the challenges many young professionals face in the modern workplace. She emphasizes the importance of awareness, listening to oneself and finding a healthy balance in the pursuit of professional success.

2.2 Lessons learned and inspiration

2.2.1 The Importance of Listening to Yourself

In the hustle and bustle of modern life, with its

incessant demands and ever-present distractions, it is easy to lose sight of our own needs and feelings. We are often pushed to ignore the warning signals that our body and mind send us, favoring external expectations and short-term goals. However, as previous testimony has shown, ignoring these signals can have devastating consequences.

Listening to yourself is a subtle but essential art. This means taking the time to connect with your own emotions, recognize your limitations, and act accordingly. It is a process of introspection that requires honesty, vulnerability and courage.

Signs of fatigue, irritability, stress or anxiety are not simply obstacles to overcome, but valuable indicators of our inner state. They remind us that we are human, with needs and limits, and that it is essential to take care of ourselves.

Listening to yourself also means recognizing your own values and priorities. In a world where success is often measured in terms of wealth, status or productivity, it's crucial to remember what really matters to us. Is it time spent with family and friends? Personal achievement? Contribution to society? By identifying and honoring these values, we can create a life that is not only successful, but also meaningful.

Finally, listening to yourself is an act of self-love. This means giving yourself permission to take time for yourself, to say no when necessary, and to seek support when you need it. It is recognizing that we deserve respect, compassion and care, not only from others, but also from ourselves.

In short, listening to yourself is an essential skill for navigating today's complex and demanding world. It keeps us grounded, resilient and authentic, and is an invaluable source of inspiration and strength.

2.2.2 Establishing Boundaries

In a society where information overload, constant availability, and a culture of "more and more" are the norm, setting boundaries has become a vital necessity for our mental and emotional well-being. Boundaries are not just physical or tangible barriers; they are boundaries we put in place to protect our energy, our time, and our integrity.

1. **Understand the value of boundaries** : Boundaries are not signs of weakness or selfishness. On the contrary, they are indications of self-respect. By establishing clear boundaries, we give ourselves the space to breathe, to recharge, and to function at our best level.

2. **Recognize your own needs** : Before we can set boundaries, it is essential to understand what we need to be healthy and balanced. This might mean recognizing the need for alone time, regular breaks during the workday,

or moments of relaxation without distractions.

3. **Communicate clearly** : Once we have identified our needs, it is crucial to communicate them clearly to others. This can be uncomfortable, especially if we are not used to expressing our needs, but it is essential to being heard and respected.

4. **Learn to say no** : Saying no is one of the most powerful skills we can develop. This does not mean being intransigent or closed-minded, but rather recognizing that every time we say yes to something, we are saying no to something else. Saying no allows us to prioritize what is truly important to us.

5. **Avoid overload** : In our desire to please, be helpful or meet expectations, we can easily overload ourselves with responsibilities and commitments. Setting boundaries means recognizing our limits and avoiding stretching ourselves too thin.

6. **Seek support** : Setting boundaries can be difficult, especially if we are surrounded by people who don't respect them. In these situations, it is essential

to seek support from friends, family or professionals who can help us reinforce and maintain our boundaries.

7.   **Reassess regularly** : Our needs and circumstances can change over time. It is therefore important to regularly re-evaluate our boundaries to ensure that they are still relevant and effective.

In conclusion, setting boundaries is an act of empowerment. It allows us to take control of our lives, protect our well-being, and live in a more authentic and fulfilling way. In the context of burnout, boundaries are a lifeline, helping us navigate the stormy waters of modern life with resilience and grace.

2.2.3 The Strength of the Community

Human beings are, by nature, social beings. Since the earliest days of our existence, we have depended on groups to survive, learn and evolve. In the context of burnout, the community plays a vital role not only in prevention, but also in healing and resilience.

1.   **Emotional Support** : When we are going through difficult times, knowing that we are not alone can be a great comfort. Sharing our experiences, fears, and hopes with others can ease the burden of burnout. Simply listening empathetically to a friend or community member can have a profound impact on our

emotional well-being.

2. **Exchange of Experiences** : Each person has their own story and their own lessons learned. By sharing these experiences within a community, we can benefit from the knowledge and perspectives of others, while offering our own insights.

3. **Resources and Tools** : Within a community, it is easier to find resources, tips and tools that have helped others overcome similar challenges. Whether it's a book, a relaxation technique or a therapeutic approach, the community is often an invaluable source of information.

4. **Mutual Accountability** : When we share our goals and challenges with others, we create a sense of mutual responsibility. It can motivate us to take positive actions for our well-being, knowing that others are there to support and encourage us.

5. **Celebrating Victories** : Every small step forward is worth celebrating. Within a community, we can share our successes, no matter how small, and receive encouragement and praise that builds our confidence and motivation.

6. **Reducing Stigma** : Unfortunately, burnout and other mental health issues are often surrounded by stigma. By talking openly about these topics within a community, we can help

break down these taboos and create a more understanding and caring environment.

7. **Building Resilience** : Together we are stronger. By drawing on the collective strength of a community, we can develop resilience in the face of life's challenges, learning from each other's experiences.

In short, community is an essential pillar of healing and preventing burnout. It reminds us that we are interconnected, that our experiences have value, and that together we can overcome the toughest challenges. In an increasingly isolated and digital world, finding that sense of community is more important than ever.

2.2.4 The Redefinition of Success

In a society where success is often measured by material indicators such as salary, job position or possessions, it is easy to get lost in the relentless pursuit of these goals. However, burnout often reminds us that these external indicators do not always equate to true satisfaction or happiness. Redefining success in more personal and meaningful terms is essential for a balanced and fulfilling life.

1. **Inner vs. Outer Success** : Although society often values external achievements, true success lies in our inner state. Feeling at peace, having healthy relationships, and finding meaning in what we do are indicators of success

that are far deeper than any salary or title.

2.   **Personal Values** : Each of us has values that we hold dear. Whether it's integrity, compassion, creativity, or authenticity, aligning our actions with these values is a true measure of success. When we live in accordance with our values, we feel a deep satisfaction that goes beyond any material accomplishment.

3.   **Work/Personal Life Balance** : In the race for success, it is easy to neglect other aspects of our life, such as health, family or hobbies. Redefining success means recognizing the importance of a healthy work-life balance.

4.   **Personal Growth** : Success lies not only in achieving goals, but also in the growth and evolution we experience along the way. Every challenge, every failure and every victory contributes to our personal development.

5.   **Positive Impact** : For many, success is also measured by the positive impact we have on others and the world. Whether through our work, our relationships or our volunteer actions, leaving a positive mark is a true mark of success.

6.   **Presence and Mindfulness** : In a world in constant motion, the ability to be fully present and live in the moment is a valuable indicator of success. Mindfulness allows us to savor each moment and live a richer, deeper life.

7.   **Self-Acceptance** : Finally, true success lies

in accepting ourselves, with our strengths, our weaknesses, our successes and our failures. Knowing yourself, accepting yourself and loving yourself are the foundations of a successful life. In conclusion, redefining success requires deep introspection and awareness of what truly matters to us. It is a personal journey that leads us to recognize that true success lies in the quality of our inner life, in our relationships and in the positive impact we have on the world. In the context of burnout, this redefinition is essential to find meaning and balance in our lives.

2.2.5 Resilience in the Face of Adversity

Resilience is this remarkable ability to bounce back from challenges, adapt to adverse circumstances and continue to move forward despite obstacles. In the context of burnout, resilience is not only an admirable quality, it is a necessity. It allows us to overcome difficult times, find strength in vulnerability and transform trials into opportunities for growth.

1. **Nature of Resilience** : Contrary to popular belief, resilience is not an innate quality that one possesses or not. Rather, it is a skill that can be developed and strengthened with time and experience.

2. **Learning through Failures** : Every failure, no matter how painful, offers a learning

opportunity. Resilient people do not see failure as an end in itself, but as a step towards success. They learn from their mistakes and use those lessons to move forward.

3. **Adaptability** : Life is unpredictable. The ability to adapt to changes, whether expected or unexpected, is at the heart of resilience. This means accepting what you cannot change and focusing on what you can influence.

4. **Support Networks** : No one goes through life alone. Resilient people recognize the importance of having a strong support network, whether that be family, friends or support groups. These relationships offer comfort, guidance, and encouragement during difficult times.

5. **Positive Perspective** : Even in the darkest situations, resilient people look for the positive side. They cultivate realistic optimism, recognizing challenges while remaining hopeful for the future.

6. **Take Care of Yourself** : Resilience is also linked to physical and emotional well-being. Activities such as meditation, exercise, a balanced diet and adequate sleep are essential for maintaining good mental and physical health.

7. **Setting Boundaries** : Knowing how to say no, setting clear boundaries, and protecting your time and energy are crucial aspects of resilience.

This helps prevent burnout and ensures one has the resources needed to face challenges.

8.   **Celebrating Small Victories** : Resilience is nourished by recognizing and celebrating small victories every day. Every step forward, no matter how small, strengthens our self-confidence and our ability to overcome obstacles.

In short, resilience is that inner light that guides us through the storms of life. She reminds us that, even in the darkest times, there is always a glimmer of hope, an inner strength that we can rely on. Cultivating this resilience in the face of burnout means giving yourself the means to overcome adversity and find deep meaning and joy in life.

2.2.6 Mindfulness and Meditation

Mindfulness is an ancient practice that has its roots in Buddhist traditions. It has gained popularity in the Western world in recent decades, particularly thanks to its proven benefits for mental and physical health. In the context of burnout, mindfulness and meditation can be valuable tools to find inner balance and reconnect with yourself.

1.   **What is Mindfulness?**

Mindfulness is the art of being fully present in the moment, without judgment or distraction. It is a kind attention paid to our sensations, our thoughts and our emotions, without trying to modify them.

2. Mindfulness Meditation Meditation

is a practice that allows you to cultivate this attention. It can take many forms: sitting meditation, walking meditation, guided meditation, etc. The goal is to practice bringing your attention back to the present moment, often by focusing on breathing.

3. Benefits on Stress and Burnout

Numerous studies have shown that mindfulness meditation can significantly reduce levels of stress, anxiety and depression. It helps regulate the nervous system, reduce the production of cortisol (stress hormone) and improve the quality of sleep.

4. Improved Concentration

Regular practice of meditation strengthens the ability to concentrate and pay attention. It also allows you to develop better management of distractions, which is particularly useful in our hyper-connected world.

5. Strengthening the Body-Mind Connection

Mindfulness invites us to listen to our body, recognize its signals and respond to its needs. This can be particularly beneficial for those experiencing burnout, as it helps them identify and respond to early signs of stress and exhaustion.

6. **Development of Kindness towards Self**

Mindfulness meditation cultivates a kind attitude towards oneself. It teaches us to treat ourselves with compassion, to accept our imperfections and to recognize our intrinsic value.

7. **Presence in Relationships**

Mindfulness also improves the quality of our relationships. By being fully present to another, we can build deeper, more authentic connections.

8. **Integration into Daily Life**

The beauty of mindfulness is that it can be integrated into all activities of the day: eating, walking, working, etc. It's simply about bringing your attention back to the present moment, again and again.

In conclusion, mindfulness and meditation are much more than just relaxation techniques. They offer a path to a more balanced, more authentic and more fulfilling life. In the context of preventing and healing burnout, they are valuable allies in regaining serenity and well-being.

2.2.7 Daily Gratitude

Gratitude is a powerful emotion that reminds us of the blessings and beauties of life. It invites us to recognize and appreciate the things, large or small, that enrich our existence. In the context of burnout, where we can often feel overwhelmed by challenges and pressures, cultivating gratitude can be a lifeline, a way to find hope and positivity.

1. What is Gratitude?

Gratitude is a feeling of appreciation for something or someone who has had a positive impact on our life. It can be related to specific events, people, or simply the beauty and magic of everyday life.

2. The Benefits of Gratitude

Studies have shown that regularly practicing gratitude can improve emotional well-being, reduce stress and anxiety, strengthen the immune system, improve sleep, and even increase relationship satisfaction. .

3. Gratitude Journal

A common method for cultivating gratitude is to keep a gratitude journal. Every day, write down three things you are grateful for. This creates a positive routine and reinforces focus on the enjoyable moments in life.

4. Gratitude in Action

Beyond simple recognition, gratitude can also be expressed through actions. It could be a word of thanks, an act of kindness or an act of generosity towards others.

5. Gratitude as a Perspective

Adopting a gratitude perspective means seeing the world through a lens of gratitude. It's recognizing the beauty in the little things, finding the positive even in challenges and seeing the lessons in trials.

6. **Gratitude and Resilience**

Gratitude builds resilience by helping us see the bright side of things, even in difficult times. She reminds us that, even in adversity, there is always something to appreciate.

7. **Gratitude and Relationships**

Expressing gratitude to others strengthens bonds and creates a feeling of connection. This can transform relationships, creating an environment of mutual appreciation and support.

8. **Challenges of Gratitude**

Of course, there are days when it is difficult to feel gratitude. It's normal. The important thing is to recognize these moments and remember that gratitude is a practice, something you cultivate over time.

In short, gratitude is much more than just an emotion. It is a philosophy of life, a way of understanding the world with recognition and wonder. In the journey of healing from burnout, it offers a light, a constant reminder of the joys, loves and beauties that surround us, even in the darkest times.

2.2.8 Continuing Evolution

Continuous evolution is the process by which

we constantly seek to grow, learn and improve, both personally and professionally. It is a never-ending quest for development, fueled by curiosity, passion and the desire to realize our full potential. In the context of burnout, continuous evolution can be a powerful way to rebuild yourself, rediscover your passions and chart a new path for the future.

1. **What is Continuous Evolution?**

Continuous evolution is the belief that we can always learn, grow and improve. It's a mindset that pushes us to constantly seek opportunities for growth, whether through education, experience, or personal reflection.

2. **The Importance of Self-Assessment**

One of the first steps in continuous evolution is self-assessment. This means taking a step back, thinking about our strengths, our weaknesses, our passions and our aspirations. This is a time to be honest with ourselves and identify areas in which we want to grow.

3. **Lifelong Learning**

Continuous evolution encourages lifelong learning. This can take the form of formal training, readings, lectures, or simply enriching conversations with others.

4. **Flexibility and Adaptability**

In a constantly changing world, the ability to adapt is essential. Continuous evolution challenges us to be flexible, embrace change, and see challenges as opportunities for growth.

5. The Redefinition of Failures

Continuous evolution teaches us to see failures not as ends in themselves, but as steps on the path to success. Every failure is a lesson, a chance to learn and improve.

6. The Quest for Meaning

At the heart of continuous evolution is the quest for meaning. It is a search for purpose, passion and fulfillment that drives us to move forward, even in the face of adversity.

7. Work-Life Balance

Continuous evolution recognizes the importance of work-life balance. It is the understanding that to be truly fulfilled, we must nourish all aspects of our being.

8. Community and Mentoring

Evolution is often a shared journey. Finding a community of like-minded people or a mentor can be invaluable for advice, support and inspiration.

In conclusion, continuous evolution is a never-ending journey of self-discovery, learning and growth. In the context of burnout, it offers a perspective of hope, a light at the end of the tunnel, and the promise that no matter the challenges we face, we always have the capacity to grow, learn, and flourish. .

CHAPTER 3: MODERN HEALING METHODS

"Healing does not mean that pain never existed. It means that pain no longer controls our lives."

Unknown

3.1 Scientific and holistic approaches to healing from burnout

3.1.1 Cognitive-Behavioral Therapies (CBT)

Cognitive Behavioral Therapies, often abbreviated

CBT, are therapeutic approaches focused on understanding and modifying an individual's thoughts and behaviors. They are widely recognized for their effectiveness in the treatment of various psychological disorders, including burnout. Here is a detailed exploration of this method and its application in the context of burnout.

1. **What is CBT?**

CBT is based on the idea that our thoughts, feelings and behaviors are interconnected. If we can identify and change negative or dysfunctional thoughts, then we can influence our emotions and actions in positive ways.

2. **How does CBT work?**

During CBT sessions, patients work with a therapist to identify negative or erroneous thought patterns that contribute to their stress or burnout. Once identified, the therapist helps the patient to challenge them and replace them with more positive and realistic thoughts.

3. **CBT and Burnout**

In the context of burnout, CBT can help identify thoughts and behaviors that contribute to burnout, such as perfectionism or difficulty delegating. By changing these patterns, individuals can develop healthier strategies for managing stress at work.

4. **Common CBT Techniques**

Techniques used in CBT include cognitive restructuring, systematic desensitization, exposure and preventive response, and progressive relaxation.

5. Benefits of CBT

CBT is an evidence-based approach, meaning it has been widely studied and demonstrated to be effective. They are often short-term, focused on the present and focused on solving concrete problems.

6. Integration with other therapies

Although CBT is effective on its own, it can also be combined with other forms of therapy, such as interpersonal therapy or mindfulness meditation, for a more holistic approach to healing.

7. Find a CBT Therapist

If you are considering trying CBT for burnout, it is essential to find a therapist trained and certified in this method. Many professional associations offer directories of therapists specializing in CBT.

In conclusion, Cognitive Behavioral Therapies offer a structured, evidence-based approach to understanding and treating burnout. By identifying and changing negative thought and behavior patterns, individuals can regain a sense of control and well-being in their professional and personal lives.

3.1.2 Medication and Psychopharmacology

Psychopharmacology is the study of the use of medications to treat psychological disorders. Although burnout is not an illness in itself, its symptoms can sometimes be so severe that they require medication intervention. Here is an overview of the use of medication in the treatment of burnout.

1. **When is medication needed?**
The decision to use medication to treat burnout depends on the severity of the symptoms. In cases where burnout leads to disorders such as depression or anxiety, medication may be a viable option.

2. **Antidepressants**
People suffering from burnout may experience depressive symptoms. In these cases, antidepressants, such as selective serotonin reuptake inhibitors (SSRIs), may be prescribed. These medications can help regulate mood and reduce symptoms such as sadness or hopelessness.

3. **Anxiolytics**
Anxiety is another common symptom of burnout. Anxiolytics, such as benzodiazepines, can be used to treat acute anxiety. However, due to the risk of addiction, they are usually

prescribed for short-term use.

4. Mood stabilizers

In some cases, people may experience extreme fluctuations in mood. Mood stabilizers, such as lithium or certain anticonvulsants, can be used to regulate these fluctuations.

5. Important Considerations

·   **Side effects:** All medications have potential side effects. It is essential to discuss the benefits and risks associated with each medication with a healthcare professional.

·   **Drug Interactions:** If you are taking other medications, it is crucial to inform your doctor to avoid potentially dangerous interactions.

·   **Medical monitoring:** People on medication must be monitored regularly by a healthcare professional to monitor the effectiveness of the treatment and ensure that there are no unwanted side effects.

6. Combination Therapy

Often, medication is most effective when combined with other forms of therapy, such as cognitive-behavioral therapy or interpersonal therapy.

7. Conclusion

Medication can be a valuable tool in the treatment of burnout, particularly when symptoms are severe. However, it is essential to approach this option with caution and work closely with a healthcare professional to ensure the treatment is safe and effective.

3.1.3 Functional Medicine

Functional medicine is a holistic, patient-centered approach that aims to treat the underlying cause of diseases rather than focusing solely on the symptoms. It is based on the idea that each individual is unique and that treatments should be personalized according to the specific needs of each patient. Here is how functional medicine can be applied to the treatment of burnout.

1. **Basic Principles of Functional Medicine**

Functional medicine recognizes that internal imbalances and dysfunctions can lead to disease. It aims to restore balance and optimal function to the body by treating the root causes of health problems.

2. **Comprehensive Assessment**

Functional medicine practitioners often begin with a detailed assessment of the patient's medical history, lifestyle, diet, and environment. This helps identify factors that may contribute to burnout.

3. **Systems approach**

Functional medicine considers the body as an integrated system. Thus, rather than treating each symptom in isolation, it seeks to understand how the body's different systems interact and influence overall health.

4. Nutrition and diet Diet

plays a crucial role in functional medicine. Practitioners may recommend dietary changes to reduce inflammation, improve digestion, and support immune function, all of which can contribute to burnout.

5. Supplements and Herbs

Depending on the patient's specific needs, nutritional supplements or medicinal herbs may be recommended to support healing and restore internal balance.

6. Stress Management

Functional medicine recognizes the profound impact of stress on health. Stress management techniques, such as meditation, yoga, or deep breathing, can be incorporated into a treatment plan.

7. Detoxification

In some cases, an accumulation of toxins in the body can contribute to burnout. Functional medicine practitioners can recommend detoxification protocols to help eliminate these toxins and restore health.

8. Collaboration with other specialists

Functional medicine is often practiced in collaboration with other specialists, such as nutritionists, therapists or life coaches, to provide a comprehensive and integrated approach to wellness.

9. **Conclusion**

Functional medicine offers a personalized and holistic approach to the treatment of burnout. By focusing on the underlying cause of symptoms and treating the body as a whole, it aims to restore long-term health and well-being. For those seeking alternatives or complements to conventional treatments, functional medicine can offer effective and lasting solutions.

3.1.4 Mindfulness Practices

Mindfulness is an ancient practice that has gained popularity in the Western world in recent decades, particularly for its benefits on mental and physical health. It consists of paying kind attention to the present moment, without judgment. Here's how mindfulness can be a valuable tool in the fight against burnout.

1. **What is mindfulness?**

Mindfulness is the art of staying grounded in the present moment, observing your thoughts, emotions and sensations without judging them. It invites us to welcome each experience as it presents itself, whether pleasant or unpleasant.

2. **Mindfulness Meditation**

One of the most common ways to practice mindfulness is through meditation. It involves sitting in silence, focusing on your breathing or another anchor point, while observing the thoughts that come and go without becoming attached to them.

3. Mindfulness-Based Stress Reduction (MBSR)

The Mindfulness-Based Stress Reduction (MBSR) program was developed by Dr. Jon Kabat-Zinn. It combines mindfulness meditation and yoga to help individuals manage stress, anxiety and pain.

4. Benefits for burnout

· **Stress reduction:** Mindfulness helps regulate the stress response, thereby reducing levels of the stress hormone cortisol.

· **Improved focus:** By training the mind to stay focused on the present moment, mindfulness can improve focus and mental clarity.

· **Emotion regulation:** Regularly practicing mindfulness can help recognize and manage negative emotions, thereby reducing the risk of burnout.

5. Integration into daily life

The beauty of mindfulness is that it can be practiced anywhere, anytime. Whether walking, eating, or even working, it is possible to integrate moments of mindfulness into your day.

6. Workshops and Retreats

For those who want to deepen their practice, there are many mindfulness workshops and retreats available. These events often offer complete immersion in the practice, far from the distractions of everyday life.

7.   **Conclusion**

Faced with the accelerating pace of modern life and the increasing demands of work and personal life, mindfulness offers a haven of peace and tranquility. By cultivating an attentive and caring presence, it offers a powerful remedy against burnout, allowing everyone to regain balance and inner serenity.

3.1.5 Body Therapies

Bodywork therapies encompass a variety of techniques that use the body as the primary healing tool. They recognize the deep connection between body and mind and aim to restore balance by treating both simultaneously. Here is an overview of bodywork therapies and their role in healing burnout.

1.   **What are body therapies?**

Bodywork therapies are based on the idea that the body and mind are intrinsically linked. They use manual techniques and movements to treat physical and emotional imbalances.

2.   **Therapeutic massage**

Massage is one of the oldest forms of body therapy. It helps relax tense muscles, improves blood and lymphatic circulation, and offers relief from stress and anxiety.

3. Osteopathy

Osteopathy is a holistic approach that aims to restore balance in the body by treating musculoskeletal imbalances. It can be particularly beneficial for those who have chronic pain following burnout.

4. Yoga Therapy

Yoga therapy combines yoga postures, breathing techniques and meditation to treat both the body and mind. It can help improve flexibility, strength and body awareness, while providing tools to manage stress.

5. Biofeedback

Biofeedback is a technique that teaches individuals how to control certain bodily functions, such as heart rate or muscle tension. This can be especially helpful for those who suffer from anxiety or chronic stress.

6. Reflexology

Reflexology is based on the idea that certain areas of the foot correspond to different organs and systems of the body. By massaging these areas, one can stimulate healing and well-being throughout the body.

7. Benefits for burnout

- **Deep relaxation:** Body therapies provide deep relaxation, helping to break the cycle of chronic stress.

· **Body awareness:** They help to develop better awareness of one's own body, allowing one to recognize and act on the first signs of tension or stress.

· **Emotional release:** By working on the body, these therapies can also help release repressed or unprocessed emotions.

8. **Conclusion**

Bodywork therapies offer a holistic approach to healing, treating both the physical and emotional symptoms of burnout. By integrating these practices into a comprehensive care plan, it is possible to regain balance and inner harmony, essential for overcoming burnout and rediscovering a fulfilling life.

3.1.6 Expressive Therapies

Expressive therapies, also known as creative therapies, encompass a range of techniques that use the arts as a means of expression and healing. They offer an alternative avenue for exploring and expressing feelings, thoughts and experiences, often where words alone can fail. Here's an overview of expressive therapies and their role in healing burnout.

1. **What are expressive therapies?**

They are based on the idea that the creative process can be therapeutic. By using different artistic mediums, individuals can explore and express aspects of themselves that may be difficult to verbalize.

2. Art Therapy Art

therapy uses painting, drawing, sculpture, and other art forms to help individuals express and process their emotions. It can be particularly beneficial for those who have difficulty putting their feelings into words.

3. Music therapy

Music therapy uses music to facilitate communication, expression and healing. This may involve listening to music, playing an instrument, or singing.

4. Dance Therapy

Dance therapy uses movement to help express emotions and experiences. It can be particularly beneficial for those who feel disconnected from their body following burnout.

5. Therapeutic Writing

Therapeutic writing encourages individuals to write about their experiences and emotions. This can take the form of journals, poetry or stories.

6. Theater Therapy

Theater therapy uses role-playing, enactment and dramatization to explore and address emotional and relational issues.

7. Benefits for burnout

· **Emotional expression:** Expressive therapies provide a safe space to explore and express repressed or unprocessed emotions.

· **Stress reduction:** The creative process itself can be meditative and relaxing, helping to reduce stress and anxiety.

· **Self-esteem boost:** Creating something tangible can boost self-esteem and feelings of accomplishment.

· **Mind-body connection:** Therapies like dance therapy help reconnect with the body, which is often neglected during periods of intense stress.

8. Conclusion

Expressive therapies offer a unique and powerful approach to healing. By enabling creative expression, they offer a pathway to address the emotional and physical trauma of burnout, while building resilience and joy. For many, they can be an essential complement to other forms of treatment, providing a path to full recovery and a fulfilling life.

3.1.7 Energy Therapies

Energy therapies are based on the idea that the human body is surrounded and permeated by an energy field. When this field is unbalanced or blocked, it can lead to physical, emotional, or mental problems. Energy therapies aim to restore balance and flow of energy in the body, promoting healing and well-being. Here is an overview of energy therapies and their role in healing burnout.

1. **What are energy therapies?**

They are based on the ancient belief that the body and mind are connected through an energy system. By working on this system, one can influence physical and emotional health.

2. Reiki

Reiki is a Japanese form of energy healing where the practitioner channels universal energy to support the body's natural healing process. It is often used to reduce stress and promote relaxation.

3. Pranic Healing

Based on the Indian concept of "prana" or life force, this therapy aims to cleanse and energize the chakras or energy centers of the body, helping to remove energy blockages.

4. Acupuncture and acupressure

These traditional Chinese therapies aim to balance the flow of energy, or "qi", in the body by stimulating specific points using needles or pressure.

5. Biofeedback

Biofeedback uses electronic equipment to measure and display information about physiological functions, allowing a person to become aware of and control these functions to improve their health.

6. Benefits for burnout

·   **Stress Reduction:** Energy therapies can help calm the nervous system, thereby reducing stress and anxiety.

· **Improved mental clarity:** By balancing energy, many people experience increased mental clarity and better focus.

· **Energy Boost:** By clearing energy blockages, these therapies can help increase energy levels and combat fatigue associated with burnout.

· **Emotional Balance:** Energy therapies can help balance emotions, reducing feelings of depression or anxiety.

7. **Conclusion**

Energy therapies offer a holistic approach to healing, treating both the body and the mind. For those suffering from burnout, they can offer a valuable route to recovery, complementing other forms of treatment. By restoring energetic balance, they can help to revitalize and renew, allowing the individual to regain their vitality and joy of life.

3.1.8 Nature and Environmental Therapy

Nature has always been a source of inspiration, peace and healing for humanity. In the context of burnout, where stress and exhaustion dominate, reconnecting with nature can offer a breath of fresh air, literally and metaphorically. Environmental therapy, also known as nature therapy, encompasses a range of practices that use nature as a therapeutic tool. Here is an overview of this approach and its benefits:

1. **What is environmental therapy?**

It is a therapeutic approach that integrates outdoor activities and immersion in nature to promote healing, well-being and personal growth.

2. **Forest Bathing (Shinrin-Yoku)**

Originating in Japan, Shinrin-Yoku, or "forest bathing," involves spending time in the forest, walking slowly, breathing and fully immersing yourself in the natural environment. Studies show that this practice can reduce stress, improve mood and strengthen the immune system.

3. **Therapeutic Gardening**

Gardening is not just a physical activity; it also has therapeutic effects. Planting, watering, and watching plants grow can be a meditative and rewarding experience.

4. **Animal-Assisted Therapy**

The presence of animals, whether dogs, cats or other creatures, can have a calming and comforting effect. They offer unconditional affection and can help reduce anxiety and loneliness.

5. **Nature Retreats**

Getting away from the hustle and bustle of everyday life to spend time in natural surroundings can be invigorating. Retreats often offer activities like yoga, meditation, and hiking, which can help with relaxation and reflection.

6. **Benefits for burnout**

· **Stress Reduction:** Nature has a calming effect on the mind, helping to reduce the stress hormone cortisol.

· **Improved concentration:** Spending time outdoors can improve concentration and creativity.

· **Boosting Immunity:** Exposure to nature can strengthen the immune system, helping the body fight disease.

· **Emotional Balance:** Nature provides perspective, helping to balance emotions and provide a sense of inner peace.

7. **Conclusion**

Nature is a powerful medicine. In an increasingly urbanized and technological world, reconnecting with the earth, trees and animals can offer refuge from burnout. Environmental therapy reminds us of the importance of taking the time to breathe, to stop and appreciate the beauty around us. For those suffering from burnout, it offers a path to healing, peace and revitalization.

3.1.9 Coaching and Mentoring

Coaching and mentoring are two powerful approaches to helping individuals navigate life's challenges, including burnout. Although they are often used interchangeably, they have clear distinctions. In the context of burnout, these two methods can offer valuable support in understanding, managing and overcoming burnout.

1. **What is Coaching?**

Coaching is a professional partnership between the coach and the client. The coach helps the client identify specific goals, develop strategies and implement action plans. The process is focused on the present and the future, and aims to help the client realize their potential.

2. **What is Mentoring?**

Mentoring is a supportive relationship where an experienced individual (the mentor) offers advice, knowledge and experiences to a less experienced individual (the mentee). Mentoring often focuses on long-term professional and personal development.

3. **How Coaching and Mentoring can help overcome Burnout:**

·   **Outside Perspective:** A coach or mentor can provide an outside perspective, helping the individual see things from a different perspective.

·   **Personalized Strategies:** Each person is unique, and a coach can help develop strategies tailored to the individual's specific situation and needs.

·   **Accountability:** Having someone to hold you accountable can be a powerful motivator for change.

· **Emotional support:** Burnout can be isolating. Having a mentor or coach provides a safe space to share feelings and concerns.

4. **Specific advantages of Coaching:**

· **Setting clear goals:** A coach can help set clear, achievable goals to overcome burnout.

· **Skills development:** A coach can help develop specific skills, such as time management or conflict resolution, that can be beneficial in managing burnout.

5. **Specific benefits of Mentoring:**

· **Sharing experiences:** A mentor, having often experienced similar challenges, can share their experiences and offer practical advice.

· **Networking:** A mentor can introduce the mentee to a professional network, providing additional opportunities and resources.

6. **Conclusion:**

Burnout is a complex challenge that requires a multifaceted approach to its management. Coaching and mentoring, with their complementary approaches, can offer valuable support for those seeking to understand, manage and overcome burnout. Whether through strategic guidance or emotional support, both methods can play a crucial role in a person's healing journey.

3.2 Practical advice and exercises

3.2.1 Time Management and Prioritization

Effective time management and prioritization are essential to preventing and overcoming burnout. In our modern world, where everything seems urgent and distractions are everywhere, learning to manage your time strategically is crucial to maintaining a healthy work-life balance.

1. **Understand the value of your time:**

Every minute is precious. Realizing the value of your time is the first step in learning to manage it effectively.

2. **The two-minute rule:**

If a task takes less than two minutes to complete, do it immediately. This avoids the accumulation of small tasks that can become overwhelming.

3. **The Pomodoro technique:**

This technique involves working intensely for 25 minutes, then taking a 5-minute break. Repeat this cycle. This helps maintain a high level of concentration and prevents exhaustion.

4. **Priority List:**

Every morning, write down the three most important tasks to accomplish that day. Focus on completing them before moving on to less urgent tasks.

5. **Learn to say no:**
It is essential to recognize your limits. If you're overloaded, it's perfectly acceptable to politely decline additional tasks.

6. **Delegation:**
If certain tasks can be assigned to others, do not hesitate to delegate. This will allow you to focus on what you do best.

7. **Avoid multitasking:**
Multitasking may seem effective, but it often divides your attention and reduces your efficiency. Focus on one task at a time.

8. **Time Blocks:**
Plan your day into blocks of time dedicated to specific tasks. This helps ensure that each activity receives the attention it deserves.

9. **Rest periods:**
Just like the Pomodoro technique, be sure to schedule rest periods throughout the day to recharge your batteries.

10. **Regular reassessment:**
At the end of each week, take a moment to evaluate how you managed your time. This will help you make adjustments for the following week.

Conclusion:
Time management and prioritization are not only professional skills, but also life skills. By mastering them, you can not only avoid burnout, but also

improve your quality of life, your well-being and your satisfaction at work and in personal life.

3.2.2 Relaxation Techniques

Relaxation is an essential element in combating stress and preventing burnout. It helps reduce muscular tension, soothe the mind and restore inner balance. Here are some proven relaxation techniques that can be incorporated into daily life:

1. **Deep breathing:**
   o Sit or lie down comfortably.
   o Inhale slowly through your nose, filling your lungs with air.
   o Exhale slowly through your mouth, releasing any tension.
   o Repeat several times, focusing on the rhythm of your breathing.
2. **Meditation :**
   o Find a quiet place and sit in a comfortable position.
   o Close your eyes and focus on your breathing or a mantra.
   o Let thoughts come and go without judgment.
   o Practice regularly to improve concentration and inner peace.
3. **Visualization:**
   o Imagine a peaceful place, like a beach or a forest.
   o Visualize yourself in this place, feel the serenity and tranquility.

o Use all your senses to make the experience as real as possible.

4. **Muscle relaxation exercises:**
   o Start at the feet and work your way up.
   o Contract each muscle group for a few seconds, then release.
   o Notice the difference between tension and relaxation.

5. **Yoga:**
   o Yoga combines postures, breathing and meditation to harmonize body and mind.
   o There are many styles of yoga, find the one that suits you best.

6. **Hot baths:**
   o A warm bath can relax tense muscles and soothe the mind.
   o Add Epsom salts or essential oils for added relaxation.

7. **Music therapy:**
   o Listen to calming music or nature sounds.
   o Music has the power to change our mood and relax us deeply.

8. **Self-massage:**
   o Use your hands or massage tools to relax tense areas.
   o Focus on the neck, shoulders and back, where we often carry the most tension.

9. **Aromatherapy:**
   o Essential oils, such as lavender or chamomile, can have a calming effect.

o Diffuse them into the air or add them to a warm bath.

10. **Biofeedback techniques:**
   o These techniques use electronic equipment to teach you how to control certain bodily functions, such as muscle tension or skin temperature.
   o Over time, you can learn to achieve a relaxed state without the equipment.

Conclusion:

Relaxation is a skill that requires practice. Find the techniques that work best for you and incorporate them into your daily routine. Even just a few minutes a day can make a big difference in your overall well-being.

3.2.3 Introspective Journal

Introspective journaling is a powerful technique for exploring your thoughts, emotions and experiences. It serves as a mirror to the soul, providing a safe space for reflection, awareness and personal growth. Here's how to use introspective journaling to heal burnout and improve well-being:

1. **Understand the goal:**
   o The introspective journal is not simply a place to record the events of the day. It is a tool for deepening self-understanding, identifying thought and emotional patterns, and finding solutions to challenges.

2.   **Write regularly:**
   o Try to write in your journal every day, even if it's just for a few minutes. Regularity creates a habit that strengthens the connection with yourself.
3.   **Let your thoughts run wild:**
   o Don't censor yourself. Write down everything that comes to mind, even if it seems unimportant or incoherent. In time, patterns and revelations will emerge.
4.   **Ask yourself questions:**
   o Use your journal to ask introspective questions. "Why did I react this way today?", "What is causing me stress right now?", "What can I do to improve my situation?"
5.   **Write down your dreams:**
   o Dreams can offer valuable insights into our subconscious. By writing them down, you can begin to identify themes or messages that may be relevant to your healing.
6.   **Celebrate small victories:**
   o Use your journal to note times when you felt improvement or accomplished something positive. This can serve as a reminder of your progress.
7.   **Think about triggers:**
   o By identifying what triggers stress or anxiety, you can work to avoid or manage these situations in the future.
8.   **Visualize the future:**

o Use your journal to imagine a future without burnout. How do you feel ? What have you accomplished? This visualization can serve as motivation.

9. **Review and reflect:**

o Take the time every month or quarter to reread your previous entries. This will allow you to see your progress, identify patterns, and reflect on what you have learned.

10. **Keep it private:**

o Your journal is a personal space. Make sure it is kept in a safe place where you can write freely without fear of being judged.

Conclusion:

The introspective journal is a valuable ally in the burnout healing journey. It provides space for reflection, expression and self-discovery. By engaging in this practice regularly, one can gain clarity, perspective, and inner strength.

3.2.4 Food and Nutrition

Diet plays a crucial role in our overall well-being, influencing everything from our physical energy to our emotional balance. When we face burnout, our bodies and minds are put under intense stress, making it even more essential to provide the appropriate nutrients to support healing and resilience.

1. **Understand the link between food and mood:**

o   What we consume can directly affect our mood and energy. Nutrient-rich foods can improve brain function, increase energy levels and strengthen the immune system.

2.   **Prioritize whole foods:**

o   Opt for unprocessed foods such as vegetables, fruits, whole grains, lean proteins and healthy fats. These foods provide lasting energy and support cognitive function.

3.   **Avoid refined sugars:**

o   Rapid spikes and drops in blood sugar can lead to mood swings, fatigue, and food cravings. Reduce consumption of sugary drinks, candy and other foods high in added sugar.

4.   **Integrate omega-3:**

o   Omega-3 fatty acids, found in fatty fish like salmon, walnuts and flaxseed, are essential for brain health and can help combat depression and anxiety.

5.   **Hydration:**

o   Water is essential for all bodily functions, including digestion, temperature regulation, and nutrient transport. Make sure you drink enough water throughout the day.

6.   **Prebiotics and probiotics:**

o   Gut health is closely linked to mental health. Include probiotic-rich foods like yogurt, sauerkraut, and kimchi, and prebiotics like garlic, onion, and asparagus to support healthy gut flora.

7.   **Vitamins and minerals:**
   o   Magnesium, zinc, vitamins B and D are essential for mental health. Make sure you get these nutrients from food or consider taking supplements after consulting a healthcare professional.

8.   **Reduce caffeine:**
   o If you experience anxiety or trouble sleeping, consider reducing your caffeine intake. Opt for alternatives like green tea or herbal teas.

9.   **Listen to your body:**
   o   Each person is unique. Take note of how certain foods affect you and adjust your diet accordingly.

10.   **Consult a nutritionist:**
   o   If you're unsure or have specific dietary needs, consider consulting a nutritionist or dietitian for personalized advice.

Conclusion:

Food is one of the pillars of our well-being. By nourishing our bodies with the right nutrients, we can support our recovery from burnout, improve our mood and build our resilience to life's challenges. Adopting a mindful and balanced approach to nutrition is an essential step on the path to recovery and overall well-being.

3.2.5 Physical Activity and Movement

Physical activity is an essential part of overall health and well-being. It offers a multitude of benefits, from improving physical health to promoting mental health. For those struggling with burnout, incorporating movement into their daily routine can be a powerful tool for healing and prevention.

1. **Mental Health Benefits:**
   o Exercise releases endorphins, often called "happy hormones," which act as natural antidepressants. It can help reduce symptoms of depression, anxiety and stress.
2. **Improved sleep:**
   o Regular physical activity promotes deeper, more restful sleep, essential for mental and physical recovery.
3. **Building resilience:**
   o Regular exercise not only strengthens the body but also the mind, helping individuals better manage stress and bounce back from challenges.
4. **Mind-body connection:**
   o Practices like yoga or tai chi promote a deep connection between body and mind, helping individuals to be more present and aware of their needs.
5. **Socialization and community:**
   o Participating in group activities, like fitness classes or running clubs, provides the opportunity to socialize, bond, and find

support.

6. **Nature and the outdoors:**
   o Outdoor activities, such as hiking or cycling, allow you to connect with nature, which has been shown to have beneficial effects on mental health.
7. **Flexibility and adaptability:**
   o There is no need to engage in intense workouts. Even short walks or light stretches can have positive effects.
8. **Establish a routine:**
   o Creating a regular exercise routine can provide structure and a sense of accomplishment, boosting self-esteem.
9. **Listen to your body:**
   o It is essential to listen to your body and recognize its limits. If an activity is too intense or causes pain, it is important to adapt and choose gentler movements.
10. **Consult a professional:**
    o If you are new to exercise or have medical concerns, it may be helpful to consult a healthcare professional or personal trainer for tailored recommendations.

Conclusion:

Physical activity is much more than a way to improve physical health. It provides a space to connect with yourself, release stress and find joy in movement. By integrating physical activity into a daily routine, one can find balance, strength and resilience in the face of the challenges of burnout.

3.2.6 Restorative Sleep

Sleep is one of the fundamental pillars of health and well-being. It plays a crucial role in physical and mental regeneration, memory consolidation, emotion regulation and maintaining hormonal balance. For those struggling with burnout, quality sleep can be the key to regaining energy and vitality.

1. **Importance of sleep:**
   o Sleep allows the body and mind to repair and regenerate. It strengthens the immune system, promotes cell growth and helps with memory consolidation.
2. **Sleep cycles:**
   o Deep, restorative sleep includes several cycles, including REM sleep, essential for mental health, and deep sleep, crucial for physical recovery.
3. **Sleep hygiene:**
   o Establishing a regular routine, avoiding caffeine and screens before bed, and creating an environment conducive to sleep are essential for good sleep hygiene.
4. **The impact of stress:**
   o Stress and anxiety can disrupt sleep. Relaxation techniques, such as meditation or deep breathing, can help calm the mind before bed.

5. **Diet and sleep:**
   o Certain foods can promote better sleep. For example, foods rich in tryptophan, such as bananas or nuts, can help with the production of melatonin, the sleep hormone.

6. **Physical activity :**
   o Regular exercise can improve sleep quality, but it's best to avoid strenuous activities right before bed.

7. **Sleep environment:**
   o A dark, quiet, cool bedroom is ideal for sleep. Investing in a good mattress and comfortable pillows can also make a difference.

8. **Avoiding sleep disruptors:**
   o Caffeine, alcohol and screens emitting blue light can disrupt sleep. It is recommended to limit them, especially in the evening.

9. **Consult a specialist:**
   o If sleep problems persist, it may be helpful to see a sleep specialist to identify possible underlying problems.

10. **Nap :**
   o A short nap in the early afternoon can help recharge the batteries, but it is best to avoid sleeping too long so as not to disrupt nighttime sleep.

Conclusion:

Restorative sleep is essential for recovery from

burnout. By prioritizing sleep and adopting healthy habits, we can regain the energy, mental clarity and emotional balance needed to overcome everyday challenges.

3.2.7 Mindfulness Practices

Mindfulness is an ancient practice that has gained popularity in recent years, particularly because of its proven benefits for mental and physical health. It consists of paying kind attention to the present moment, without judgment or distraction.

1. **What is mindfulness?**
    o Mindfulness is the art of being fully present and engaged in the moment, without being distracted by passing thoughts or judgments.
2. **Mindfulness meditation:**
    o It is a technique which consists of concentrating on one's breathing, one's bodily sensations or an object of meditation, while observing the thoughts and emotions which arise, without attaching to them.
3. **Mental health benefits:**
    o Regularly practicing mindfulness can reduce stress, anxiety, and depressive symptoms. It also promotes better emotional regulation and greater mental clarity.
4. **Daily applications:**
    o Mindfulness can be integrated into daily activities, such as eating, walking, or

listening. It's about fully engaging in the activity, paying attention to every sensation and experience.

5. **Mindfulness at work:**
   o Short, regular breaks to practice mindfulness can help you stay focused, reduce stress and improve productivity.

6. **Simple exercises:**
   o Conscious breathing, observing body sensations or guided meditation are simple exercises that can be practiced anywhere and at any time.

7. **Apps and resources:**
   o There are many apps and online resources to guide beginners in their mindfulness practice, such as "Headspace" or "Calm."

8. **Workshops and retreats:**
   o For those who want to deepen their practice, there are mindfulness workshops and retreats that offer complete immersion in this discipline.

9. **Mindfulness for children:**
   o Introducing mindfulness from a young age can help children manage their emotions, improve their concentration and develop better self-esteem.

10. **Limitations and precautions:**
   o Although beneficial for many, mindfulness is not a silver bullet and does not replace medical or therapeutic treatment. It is

important to listen to your body and consult a professional if necessary.

Conclusion:

Mindfulness is a powerful tool for improving mental and physical well-being. By cultivating an attentive presence in the present moment, we can develop greater resilience in the face of life's challenges and find inner balance. For those suffering from burnout, it's a practice that can offer respite and a new perspective on life.

3.2.8 Social Connection

Social connectedness refers to the quality and quantity of relationships we have with others. It is essential to our emotional, mental and physical well-being. In the context of burnout, social connection can play a crucial role in prevention, recovery and resilience.

1. **Importance of Social Connection:**
   - Human beings are social creatures by nature. Our well-being is closely linked to the quality of our relationships. Strong social connection can strengthen our immune systems, reduce stress and increase longevity.
2. **Isolation vs Connection:**
   - Social isolation can exacerbate burnout symptoms. Feeling alone or misunderstood can increase stress, anxiety and depression. Conversely, being surrounded by caring and understanding people can provide much-

needed emotional support.

3. **Create authentic connections:**
   - o   It's not just about the quantity, but the quality of relationships. Seek authentic, deep, meaningful interactions rather than superficial relationships.

4. **Support groups:**
   - o   Joining support groups for burnout or other mental health challenges can provide a platform to share experiences, advice and find understanding.

5. **Social activities :**
   - o   Engage in activities that promote connection, such as clubs, hobby groups, or community events. These activities can help build new relationships and strengthen existing ones.

6. **Technology and connection:**
   - o   Although technology can sometimes contribute to isolation, it also offers ways to connect. Video calls, online groups and social apps can help maintain connection, especially during times of social distancing.

7. **Limitations of social networks:**
   - o   While social media can offer a form of connection, it can also contribute to feelings of comparison, inadequacy, or isolation. It is essential to use them wisely.

8. **Establish boundaries:**
   - o   While seeking connection, it is also crucial

to establish healthy boundaries to avoid emotional burnout or toxic relationships.

9. **Connection with yourself:**
   o Along with connecting with others, it is essential to cultivate a healthy relationship with yourself. Meditation, mindfulness, and self-reflection can help strengthen this inner connection.

Conclusion:

Social connection is a pillar of human well-being. In the burnout healing journey, it can offer the support, understanding and strength needed to overcome challenges and regain balance. By cultivating healthy relationships and seeking authentic connections, we can enrich our lives and strengthen our resilience in the face of challenges.

3.2.9 Healthy Working Environment

The work environment plays a crucial role in our overall well-being, especially when you consider the considerable amount of time we spend there. A healthy work environment can not only prevent burnout, but also promote productivity, creativity and general well-being.

1. **Physical Spaces:**
   o **Ergonomics:** Having an ergonomic workspace reduces the risk of musculoskeletal pain and promotes comfort throughout the day.
   o **Natural Light:** Daylight can improve mood, productivity and reduce eye strain.

- o **Green Spaces:** Plants or a view of nature can reduce stress and improve air quality.

2. **Corporate culture :**
   - o **Recognition:** Feeling valued and recognized for your work strengthens morale and motivation.
   - o **Open Communication:** Promote an open dialogue where employees feel listened to and understood.
   - o **Work-life balance:** Encourage employees to take time for themselves and respect their rest hours.

3. **Stress management :**
   - o **Training:** Offer training on stress management and resilience.
   - o **Relaxation Spaces:** Create areas where employees can relax, meditate or even take a nap.

4. **Flexibility:**
   - o **Telecommuting:** Providing the ability to work remotely can reduce travel stress and provide a better work-life balance.
   - o **Flexible Schedules:** Allow employees to adapt their schedules according to their personal needs.

5. **Professional relationships :**
   - o **Team Building:** Organize activities to strengthen team spirit and improve relationships between colleagues.
   - o **Conflict Management:** Have procedures in

place to resolve conflicts constructively.

6. **Professional Development:**
   - o **Continuing Education:** Provide training opportunities so employees can continue to grow and learn.
   - o **Constructive Feedback:** Provide regular feedback to help employees improve and grow.
7. **Health and wellbeing :**
   - o **Wellness Programs:** Offer programs that encourage physical, mental and emotional health, such as yoga classes, meditation or stress management workshops.
   - o **Access to Counselors:** Provide access to mental health professionals to support employees with their personal and professional challenges.

Conclusion:

A healthy work environment goes far beyond an ergonomic desk. It encompasses company culture, co-worker relationships, stress management and much more. By investing in a healthy work environment, companies can not only prevent burnout, but also attract and retain the best talent, while promoting productivity and employee satisfaction.

3.2.10 Digital Disconnect

In the digital age, where technology is omnipresent, digital disconnection has become an essential element in preserving our mental and emotional well-being. Here is why and how to implement this life-saving practice:

1. **The Impact of Overconnection:**
   o **Mental Fatigue:** Constant demand from notifications, emails and messages can lead to cognitive overload.
   o **Sleep Disruption:** Exposure to blue light from screens before sleeping can disrupt the production of melatonin, a sleep-regulating hormone.
   o **Affected Social Relations:** Excessive use of digital devices can decrease the quality of direct human interactions.
2. **The Benefits of Disconnection:**
   o **Mental Revitalization:** Taking a break from screens allows the mind to regenerate.
   o **Improved Concentration:** Without constant distractions, one can focus more deeply on a task.
   o **Strengthening Social Connections:** Spending quality time without digital distractions strengthens relationships.
3. **Strategies for Effective Disconnection:**
   o **Screen-Free Time:** Establish specific screen-free times of the day, such as during meals or before bed.
   o **Digital Vacation:** Take days where you completely disconnect, without emails, without social media.
   o **Minimal Notifications:** Turn off non-essential notifications to reduce

interruptions.

4. **Tools and Applications:**
   - o **Wellness Apps:** Use apps that encourage regular breaks from screens or track time spent on devices.
   - o **Do Not Disturb Mode:** Activate this mode during busy work or rest hours to minimize distractions.
5. **Education and Awareness:**
   - o **Workshops and Training:** Organize sessions to raise awareness among employees or family members of the importance of disconnection.
   - o **Literature and Resources:** Encourage the reading of books or articles on the benefits of digital disconnection.
6. **Create a Favorable Environment:**
   - o **Screen-Free Zones:** Establish areas in the home or work where digital devices are not allowed.
   - o **Disconnection Rituals:** Establish rituals, such as a walk after dinner without a phone or a moment of meditation without digital distractions.

Conclusion:

Digital disconnection is not a rejection of technology, but a balanced approach to enjoying it while preserving our well-being. In a world where the line between work and personal life is increasingly blurred, it is essential to take the time to disconnect, recharge and reconnect with what really matters.

3.2.11 Importance of digital breaks

In an age where technology is deeply integrated into our daily lives, digital breaks have become a necessity for maintaining a healthy work-life balance. Here's why these breaks are essential and how they can transform our well-being:

1. **Information Overload:**
   - **Cognitive Saturation:** Constant consumption of information, whether through news, social media, or email, can lead to mental saturation.
   - **Reduced Productivity:** Constant stimulation can decrease our ability to focus on specific tasks.
2. **Health Effects:**
   - **Stress and Anxiety:** The perceived need to be constantly connected can increase stress and anxiety levels.
   - **Eye Fatigue:** Prolonged fixation on screens can cause eye fatigue, headaches and blurred vision.
3. **Quality of Relationships:**
   - **Superficial Interactions:** Excessive device use can lead to less meaningful and more superficial interactions with loved ones.
   - **Absent Presence:** Being physically present but mentally distracted by digital devices can harm the quality of relationships.

4. **Benefits of Digital Breaks:**
   o **Mental Invigoration:** Disconnecting, even briefly, allows the mind to rest and regenerate.
   o **Enhanced Creativity:** Getting away from digital distractions can boost creative thinking and problem solving.
   o **Strengthening Human Connections:** Spending time without digital distractions promotes deeper, more meaningful interactions.

5. **Implementation of Digital Breaks:**
   o **Scheduling:** Set specific times of day to unplug, such as for an hour after lunch or before bed.
   o **Substitution Activities:** Replace screen time with enriching activities like reading, meditation, or walks in nature.
   o **Disconnection Challenges:** Set up personal or group challenges, such as a screen-free day once a week.

6. **Awareness and Education:**
   o **Get informed:** Understand the negative effects of overuse of digital devices on mental and physical health.
   o **Workshops and Seminars:** Participate in educational sessions on the importance of digital breaks and their benefits.

Conclusion:

Digital breaks are not a luxury, but a necessity in our hyperconnected world. They offer a breath of fresh air to our minds, strengthen our relationships and improve our overall well-being. Adopting this practice can transform our relationship with technology and enrich our quality of life.

3.2.12 Tips for healthy use of technologies

Technology, while beneficial in many ways, can also have detrimental effects on our well-being if not used wisely. Here are some tips for healthy and balanced use of technologies:

1. **Establish Time Limits:**
   o **Fixed Times:** Allocate specific periods to check your emails, social media or other apps to avoid excessive usage.
   o **Alarms and Reminders:** Use alarms to limit the time spent on certain apps or websites.
2. **Technology-Free Spaces:**
   o **Screen-Free Zones:** Create areas in your home, such as the bedroom or dining room, where electronic devices are prohibited.
   o **Technology-Free Time:** Create times, like family meals, without digital distractions.
3. **Conscious Use:**
   o **Ask yourself:** Before picking up your phone, ask yourself: "Do I really need this right now?"
   o **Airplane Mode:** Use airplane mode during times when you want to concentrate or rest.

4.   **Wellness Applications:**
   o **Screen Time Tracking:** Use apps that track time spent on your phone or computer.
   o **Meditation Apps:** Integrate apps that encourage mindfulness and relaxation.
5.   **Visual Hygiene:**
   o **Adapted Brightness:** Adjust the brightness of your devices according to the ambient lighting.
   o **Night Mode:** Use night mode or blue light filters to reduce eye strain.
6.   **Digital Detox:**
   o **Technology-Free Days:** Dedicate one day per week or month to completely disconnecting.
   o **Digital Vacation:** When you go on vacation, limit the use of technology to reconnect with nature and your loved ones.
7.   **Education and Awareness:**
   o **Understand the Risks:** Educate yourself about the potential dangers of excessive technology use, such as digital burnout or addiction.
   o **Workshops and Training:** Participate in workshops that teach healthy use of technology.
8.   **Prioritize Human Connections:**
   o **Face-to-Face Interactions:** Prioritize direct interactions over digital communications.
   o **Offline Activities:** Engage in activities

that don't require devices, such as reading, sports, or art.

9.   **Update and Cleanup:**

o **Uninstall:** Remove unused or distracting apps regularly.

o **Notifications:** Turn off non-essential notifications to reduce distractions.

Conclusion:

Healthy use of technology requires awareness and discipline. By setting boundaries and prioritizing our well-being, we can enjoy the benefits of technology while maintaining our mental and physical health.

CHAPTER 4: WELLBEING TRENDS FOR 2024

4.1 The latest wellness trends and how they can help with burnout recovery

4.1.1 Technology and Well-being

Technology has always been at the forefront of transforming our society, and the field of wellness is no exception. In 2024, technology will play a crucial role in how we approach and integrate well-being into our daily lives. Here's how :

1. **Meditation and Mindfulness Applications:**
   o **Virtual Guidance:** Apps like "Calm" and "Headspace" offer guided sessions to help users refocus, reduce stress and improve concentration.
   o **Personalization:** These apps use AI to recommend sessions based on the user's mood and needs.
2. **Wellness Wearables:**
   o **Continuous Tracking:** Smartwatches and fitness bands track everything from sleep quality to heart rate, providing real-time health insights.
   o **Relaxation Alerts:** These devices can send reminders to take breaks, meditate, or even take deep breaths when they detect high levels of stress.
3. **Virtual Reality (VR) for Relaxation:**
   o **Virtual Escapes:** VR allows users to escape to peaceful environments, such as a beach or forest, providing a break from the daily hustle and bustle.
   o **VR Therapy:** Some therapists use VR to treat issues like anxiety or PTSD.
4. **Online Fitness Platforms:**
   o **Virtual Classes:** Platforms like "Peloton" or "Mirror" offer live and on-demand fitness classes, allowing people to stay active at home.

- o **Online Communities:** These platforms also offer a sense of community, where users can connect and support each other.
5. **Nutrition Tracking Applications:**
   - o **Food Diary:** Apps like "MyFitnessPal" allow users to track their food intake and get nutrient information.
   - o **Food Recommendations:** Based on the user's health goals, these apps can suggest meals and recipes.
6. **Digital Therapy:**
   - o **Easy Access:** Platforms like "Talkspace" or "BetterHelp" connect users to licensed therapists via chats, video calls or messages.
   - o **Anonymity:** For those who prefer discretion, these platforms provide a safe space to discuss issues without judgment.

Conclusion:

Technology, when used wisely, can be a powerful tool for improving well-being. In 2024, with the rise of technological innovations, it will be easier than ever to integrate wellness practices into our daily lives, helping to prevent and cure burnout.

4.1.2 Wellness Retreats

As modern life becomes more and more hectic, the need to unplug and refocus has never been more crucial. Wellness retreats, which have seen a surge in popularity in 2023, provide that much-sought-after escape. Here is an overview of this trend and its benefits:

1. **Escape from Routine:**
   - o **Digital Disconnect:** These retreats often encourage a complete disconnect from electronic devices, allowing participants to take a break from information overload.
   - o **Back to Nature:** Many of these retreats are located in natural environments, such as mountains, forests or beaches, offering communion with nature.
2. **Holistic Practices:**
   - o **Yoga and Meditation:** These sessions help improve flexibility, strength and self-awareness.
   - o **Alternative Therapies:** Practices such as aromatherapy, reflexology and acupuncture are often offered to revitalize the body and mind.
3. **Conscious Nutrition:**
   - o **Organic Food:** The meals served are often organic, local and adapted to the nutritional needs of participants.
   - o **Cooking Workshops:** Some offer workshops where participants can learn how to prepare healthy meals.
4. **Personal development :**
   - o **Workshops and Seminars:** Experts offer sessions on topics such as stress management, mindfulness and emotional communication.
   - o **Journaling Practices:** Participants are

encouraged to keep a journal to reflect on their experiences and feelings.

5. **Physical activity :**
   - o **Hiking and Excursions:** Outdoor activities, such as hiking, canoeing or horseback riding, are common.
   - o **Water Sports:** For waterside retreats, activities like swimming, paddleboarding or snorkeling are popular.

6. **Community and Connection:**
   - o **Sharing Circles:** Safe spaces where participants can share their experiences and feelings.
   - o **Group Activities:** Activities like campfires, dancing or singing strengthen the feeling of community.

Conclusion:

Wellness retreats in 2023 are not just a trend, but a response to the growing need to reconnect with yourself in an ever-changing world. They offer a unique combination of relaxation, revitalization and reflection, allowing participants to return to their daily lives with a refreshed perspective and renewed energy.

4.1.3 Alternative Therapies

In the context of wellness in 2024, alternative therapies have gained popularity as supplements or sometimes even alternatives to traditional medical methods. These therapies emphasize a holistic approach to health, considering the individual as a whole: body, mind and soul. Here is an overview of the hottest alternative therapies for 2024:

1. **Acupuncture and Acupressure:**
   - **Principle:** Based on traditional Chinese medicine, these therapies aim to balance the flow of energy (Qi) in the body by stimulating specific points.
   - **Benefits:** Pain relief, stress reduction, improved digestion and strengthened immune system.
2. **Aromatherapy:**
   - **Principle:** Use of essential oils extracted from plants to promote physical and emotional health.
   - **Benefits:** Reduced anxiety, improved sleep, boosted immunity and headache relief.
3. **Reflexology:**
   - **Principle:** Stimulation of specific points on the feet, hands and ears to influence other parts of the body.
   - **Benefits:** Stress relief, improved blood circulation and balancing bodily functions.
4. **Crystal Therapy:**
   - **Principle:** Use of stones and crystals to balance and harmonize the body's energies.
   - **Benefits:** Strengthening mental clarity, improving energy and balancing the chakras.
5. **Reiki:**

o   **Principle:** Japanese energy healing technique where the practitioner channels universal energy to promote healing and balance.

o   **Benefits:** Reduction of stress, promotion of relaxation and improvement of general well-being.

6.   **Biofeedback:**

o   **Principle:** Technique that teaches how to control physiological functions to improve performance, health and well-being.

o   **Benefits:** Stress management, reduction of anxiety and improvement of concentration.

7.   **Sound Therapy:**

o   **Principle:** Using sound vibrations (like Tibetan bowls or tuning forks) to promote healing and balance.

o   **Benefits:** Improved concentration, reduced stress and promoted deep relaxation.

Conclusion:

In 2024, faced with the accelerating pace of life and increasing mental health challenges, alternative therapies offer a breath of fresh air. They remind us of the importance of considering the individual as a whole and seeking solutions outside traditional frameworks. These therapies, although different in their approach, share a common objective: to promote a state of well-being and inner balance.

4.1.4 Food and Supplements

As we enter 2024, the relationship between food, supplements and wellness has been profoundly re-examined. The realization that "we are what we eat" has never been more relevant. Here's how food and supplements have become essential pillars of modern wellness:

1. **Intuitive Eating:**
    o **Principle:** Listen and respond to your body's signals of hunger and satiety rather than following restrictive diets.
    o **Benefits:** Improved relationship with food, reduced stress associated with eating and promotion of a positive body image.
2. **Superfoods:**
    o **Examples:** Acai berries, chia seeds, turmeric, spirulina.
    o **Benefits:** These foods are nutrient-dense and offer a variety of health benefits, from fighting inflammation to promoting heart health.
3. **Probiotics and Intestinal Health:**
    o **Principle:** Consumption of beneficial bacteria to promote healthy intestinal flora.
    o **Benefits:** Improved digestion, strengthening the immune system and promoting mental health (gut-brain connection).
4. **Adaptogens:**
    o **Examples:** Ashwagandha, Rhodiola, Ginseng.
    o **Benefits:** These herbs and roots help the

body adapt to stress and restore natural balance.

5. **Collagen:**
   - o **Principle:** Protein naturally present in the body, often taken in supplement form for skin, hair and joint health.
   - o **Benefits:** Improved skin elasticity, strengthened hair and nails, and joint support.

6. **Fermented Foods:**
   - o **Examples:** Kombucha, kimchi, yogurt.
   - o **Benefits:** A natural source of probiotics, these foods support gut health and strengthen the immune system.

7. **Genetically Based Diets:**
   - o **Principle:** Adapt your diet according to your genetic profile to optimize health.
   - o **Benefits:** Personalization of diet to meet the specific needs of the individual, reduction of disease risks and improvement of physical performance.

Conclusion:

In 2024, food will no longer just be seen as a source of energy, but as medicine in itself. Individuals are increasingly aware of the impact of their food choices on their overall well-being. Supplements, on the other hand, offer targeted ways to fill nutritional gaps and optimize health. The trend is clear: a proactive and personalized approach to nutrition is the key to a healthy and balanced life.

4.1.5 Food and Supplements

In 2024, the way we perceive and consume food and supplements will evolve to become a central part of our well-being. Here are some key trends and developments in this area:

1. **Personalized Power:**
   - **Principle:** Adapt your diet according to your individual needs, preferences and health goals.
   - **Benefits:** Better digestion, increased energy, reduced food intolerances and improved overall health.
2. **Nootropic Supplements:**
   - **Examples:** L-theanine, Bacopa monnieri, Rhodiola rosea.
   - **Benefits:** Improved concentration, memory and mental clarity. These supplements are designed to optimize cognitive performance.
3. **Functional Foods:**
   - **Examples:** Chia seeds, turmeric, goji berries.
   - **Benefits:** These foods offer additional nutritional benefits that can help prevent or treat illnesses and conditions.
4. **Microbiome and Probiotics:**
   - **Principle:** Support intestinal health through the consumption of beneficial bacteria.
   - **Benefits:** Improved digestion, strengthening of the immune system and potential

positive impact on mood and mental health.

5. **Alternative Proteins:**
    o **Examples:** Plant-based proteins, insects, algae.
    o **Benefits:** Offer sustainable and nutritious alternatives to traditional meat, responding to environmental and ethical concerns.

6. **Adaptogenic Supplements:**
    o **Examples:** Ashwagandha, Cordyceps, Reishi.
    o **Benefits:** Help the body adapt to stress, balance hormones and improve general vitality.

7. **Intermittent Fasting and Associated Supplements:**
    o **Principle:** Eat during a specific window of time and fast for the rest of the day.
    o **Benefits:** Weight loss, improved insulin sensitivity and increased longevity.

Bottom line:

Food and supplements have become much more than just sources of energy or nutrients. They are now considered essential tools for optimizing health, preventing disease and improving quality of life. In 2024, thanks to scientific advances and increased awareness, individuals will be better equipped to make informed choices that support their well-being at all levels.

4.1.6 Innovative Workspaces

As we enter 2024, the world of work has

undergone major transformations, largely driven by lessons learned from the global pandemic and the rapid evolution of technology. Workspaces are no longer simply places where tasks are carried out; they have become environments designed for well-being, creativity and collaboration. Here are some notable trends in innovative workspace design:

1. **Modular Desks:**
   o **Principle:** Flexible spaces that can be adapted according to current needs.
   o **Benefits:** Promotes collaboration, provides private spaces for concentration and allows optimal use of space.
2. **Integrated Green Spaces:**
   o **Examples:** Interior gardens, green walls, terraces.
   o **Benefits:** Improved air quality, reduced stress, stimulated creativity and increased general well-being.
3. **Advanced Technology:**
   o **Examples:** Adaptive lighting systems, adjustable desks, virtual collaboration tools.
   o **Benefits:** Increased productivity, improved comfort and adaptation to the individual needs of employees.
4. **Relaxation and Meditation Spaces:**
   o **Principle:** Areas dedicated to relaxation, meditation or even naps.
   o **Benefits:** Stress reduction, improved

concentration and promotion of mental health.

5. **Biophilic Design:**
   - o **Principle:** Integrate natural elements into the design of workspaces.
   - o **Benefits:** Create a feeling of connection with nature, reduce anxiety and increase well-being.

6. **Community Spaces:**
   - o **Examples:** Collaborative cafes, play areas, informal discussion spaces.
   - o **Benefits:** Promote collaboration, strengthen corporate culture and encourage social interactions.

7. **Acoustic Solutions:**
   - o **Principle:** Use of specific materials and designs to control the sound level.
   - o **Benefits:** Reduced distractions, improved concentration and created a more pleasant working environment.

Conclusion:

The workspaces of 2024 will reflect a growing awareness of the importance of well-being at work. By incorporating natural elements, using technology wisely, and creating flexible spaces, companies are showing that they value their employees not only as workers, but also as individuals. These innovations in workspace design are a step forward in creating environments where people can thrive both professionally and personally.

4.1.7 Online Support Communities

In the digital age of 2024, the notion of community has evolved to encompass not only physical interactions but also virtual connections. Online support communities have become essential pillars for many people seeking to overcome challenges, including burnout. Here's a look at these communities and their impact:

1. **Forums and Discussion Groups:**
   - **Principle:** Platforms where individuals can share their experiences, ask questions and get answers from people who have experienced similar situations.
   - **Benefits:** Sense of belonging, reduction of isolation, access to information and practical advice.
2. **Well-being and Meditation Applications:**
   - **Examples:** Headspace, Calm, Insight Timer.
   - **Benefits:** Relaxation techniques, guided sessions, user communities sharing tips and experiences.
3. **Thematic Social Networks:**
   - **Principle:** Platforms dedicated to specific subjects, such as mental well-being, physical health or stress management.
   - **Benefits:** Targeted content, interactions with experts, support from peers sharing the same concerns.
4. **Webinars and Online Workshops:**

- o **Examples:** Live sessions with therapists, coaches or wellness experts.
- o **Benefits:** Interactive learning, acquisition of new skills, feeling of connection with a group.

5. **Virtual Support Groups:**
- o **Principle:** Regular meetings via platforms like Zoom or Teams, where members can discuss their challenges and progress.
- o **Benefits:** Constant support, mutual accountability, deep and meaningful exchanges.

6. **Online Coaching Platforms:**
- o **Examples:** BetterHelp, Talkspace.
- o **Benefits:** Access to qualified professionals, personalized sessions, flexibility and convenience.

Bottom Line:

Online support communities offer a wealth of opportunities for those seeking to understand, manage, and overcome burnout. They provide a safe space to share, learn and grow. In 2024, with technology playing an increasingly central role in our lives, these virtual communities will be more relevant than ever, providing accessible support anytime, anywhere.

4.1.8 Advanced Mindfulness Practices

Mindfulness is not new for 2024, but the methods and approaches have evolved to adapt to our constantly changing world. Advanced mindfulness practices integrate traditional techniques with the latest scientific and technological discoveries to deliver deeper, personalized experiences. Here is an overview of these advanced practices:

1. **Meditative Virtual Reality:**
   - **Principle:** Use of virtual reality to immerse the individual in peaceful environments conducive to meditation.
   - **Benefits:** Allows a total disconnection from the external environment, reinforcing concentration and immersion in the practice.
2. **Biofeedback and Neurofeedback:**
   - **Principle:** Using sensors to measure brain activity, heart rate or other physiological indicators during meditation.
   - **Benefits:** Offers real-time feedback on the state of relaxation or concentration, allowing practice to be adjusted accordingly.
3. **AI-Based Meditation Apps:**
   - **Examples:** Applications that tailor meditation sessions based on the user's needs and emotional responses.
   - **Benefits:** Personalized sessions, adapted to the specific needs of each individual.
4. **Advanced Moving Meditation:**
   - **Principle:** Integration of mindfulness into physical activities such as yoga, dance or martial arts.

o   **Benefits:** Connects body and mind, strengthens presence and body awareness.

5.   **Immersive Sound Practices:**
   o **Examples:** Sound baths, meditation with Tibetan bowls or gongs.
   o   **Benefits:** Sound frequencies can help induce states of deep relaxation and balance energies.

6.   **Quantum Meditation:**
   o **Principle:** Integrating the principles of quantum physics into meditative practice to explore the connection between consciousness and the universe.
   o **Benefits:** Broadens perspective, promotes a deeper understanding of reality.

Conclusion:

In 2024, mindfulness will cross new frontiers, integrating technology, science and spirituality to deliver deeper, transformative experiences. These advanced practices meet the needs of a modern society seeking inner peace, connection and understanding in an ever-changing world.

4.1.9 Nature and Green Therapies

Nature has always been a source of healing and well-being for humanity. In 2024, in the face of increasing urbanization and disconnection from nature, green therapies will gain popularity as a way to restore balance, reduce stress and improve mental health. Here is an overview of trends in nature and green therapies:

1. **Forest Bathing (Shinrin-Yoku):**
   - o **Principle:** Originating in Japan, this practice encourages individuals to spend time in the forest, walk slowly, breathe deeply, and fully immerse themselves in the natural environment.
   - o **Benefits:** Reduced stress, improved mood, strengthened immune system and increased concentration.
2. **Garden therapy:**
   - o **Principle:** Using gardening as a therapeutic means to improve mental and physical health.
   - o **Benefits:** Improved fine motor skills, strengthened connection to the earth, reduced anxiety and promoted relaxation.
3. **Nature Retreats:**
   - o **Examples:** Stays in eco-lodges, mountain yoga retreats or meditation by a lake.
   - o **Benefits:** Disconnection from modern distractions, immersion in the tranquility of nature, revitalization of the mind and body.
4. **Animal Therapies:**
   - o **Principle:** Interaction with animals, such as horses, dogs or cats, in a therapeutic setting.
   - o **Benefits:** Improved communication, increased self-confidence, reduced isolation and improved mental health.
5. **Meditative Walks:**

o **Principle:** Walk slowly in nature while practicing mindfulness.

o **Benefits:** Increased body awareness, improved concentration, reduced stress and strengthened connection to nature.

6. **Biophilic Architecture:**

o **Principle:** Design of buildings and spaces that integrate natural elements and promote connection to nature.

o **Benefits:** Improved occupant well-being, reduced stress, increased productivity and improved air quality.

Conclusion:

In 2024, awareness of the importance of nature for human well-being will be stronger than ever. Green therapies offer a holistic response to the challenges of modern life, recognizing the healing power of nature and integrating its benefits into our daily lives. These practices encourage a more balanced life, in harmony with our natural environment.

4.1.10 Education and Workshops

In the information age, education and workshops play a vital role in promoting well-being and preventing burnout. By 2024, with the rise of technology and growing recognition of the importance of mental well-being, educational initiatives focused on well-being will have gained momentum. Here's a look at trends in wellness education and workshops:

1. **Mindfulness Workshops:**
   - o **Principle:** These workshops teach meditation and mindfulness techniques to help participants live in the present moment, reduce stress and improve concentration.
   - o **Benefits:** Reduction of anxiety, improvement of sleep quality, strengthening of emotional resilience.
2. **Stress Management Seminars:**
   - o **Principle:** These seminars offer tools and techniques to effectively manage daily stress, whether at work or in personal life.
   - o **Benefits:** Increased productivity, improved interpersonal relationships, prevention of burnout.
3. **Holistic Nutrition Workshops:**
   - o **Principle:** These workshops focus on the importance of a balanced diet for overall well-being, with an emphasis on whole, natural and nutritious foods.
   - o **Benefits:** Improved physical health, increased energy, prevention of chronic diseases.
4. **Yoga and Tai Chi classes:**
   - o **Principle:** These classes combine physical movements with mental focus to improve flexibility, strength and inner peace.
   - o **Benefits:** Reduced stress, improved posture, strengthened mind-body connection.

5. **Effective Communication Workshops:**
   o **Principle:** These workshops teach communication techniques to improve personal and professional interactions.
   o **Benefits:** Strengthening relationships, preventing conflicts, improving collaboration.
6. **Sleep Seminars:**
   o **Principle:** These seminars offer tips and techniques to improve sleep quality, recognizing the importance of rest for mental and physical health.
   o **Benefits:** Improved concentration, reduction of fatigue, strengthening of the immune system.

Conclusion:

By 2024, wellness-focused education and workshops will have become essential components in helping individuals navigate an ever-changing world. These initiatives offer valuable tools and resources to improve quality of life, prevent burnout and promote robust mental health.

4.1.11 Modern Body Practices

In the contemporary era, awareness of the importance of bodily health has led to the emergence of new bodily practices. These methods, although modern, are often inspired by ancient traditions, while integrating the technological and scientific advances of our time.

Here is an overview of modern body practices that will be popular in 2024:

1. **Aerial Yoga:**
    o **Principle:** Use of suspended hammocks to perform yoga postures. This method allows greater freedom of movement and decompression of the spine.
    o **Benefits:** Improved flexibility, muscle strengthening, relief of back pain.

2. **Body Biohacking:**
    o **Principle:** Using technology and science to "hack" or optimize bodily functions. This may include implants, supplements, or specific breathing techniques.
    o **Benefits:** Increased energy, improved concentration, optimization of overall health.

3. **Virtual Reality Meditation:**
    o **Principle:** Use of virtual reality to create immersive environments conducive to meditation.
    o **Benefits:** Reduced stress, improved mindfulness, deep meditation experience.

4. **Gyrotonic:**
    o **Principle:** A method of exercise that combines the movements of yoga, dance, tai chi and gymnastics, often practiced with specialized equipment.
    o **Benefits:** Muscle strengthening, improved flexibility, harmonization of body and

mind.

5. **Sound Baths and Frequency Therapy:**
   - **Principle:** Using singing bowls, gongs and other instruments to create sound vibrations that have a therapeutic impact on the body.
   - **Benefits:** Deep relaxation, chakra balancing, improved mental health.

6. **Cryotherapy:**
   - **Principle:** Exposing the body to extremely low temperatures for short periods of time to stimulate blood circulation and reduce inflammation.
   - **Benefits:** Muscle recovery, improved circulation, strengthening of the immune system.

Conclusion:

Modern bodywork practices for 2024 offer a unique fusion of ancient traditions and innovative technologies. They recognize the importance of a holistic approach to health, integrating body, mind and soul to achieve optimal well-being. These methods, adapted to the needs of the modern individual, are essential for navigating an ever-changing world and for dealing with the challenges of burnout and stress.

4.2 Advice specific to the year 2024

4.2.1 Adaptation to the New Post-Pandemic Normal

The year 2024 will mark a period of transition and adaptation following the global upheaval caused by the pandemic. Although the world has begun to recover and adapt to a new reality, the impacts of the pandemic are still palpable in many aspects of daily life. Here's how to adapt to this new post-pandemic normal:

1. **Recognition of Trauma:**
   o **Principle:** It is essential to recognize that almost everyone has been affected in some way by the pandemic. This may include the loss of loved ones, career changes, or mental health challenges.
   o **Action:** Seek professional support if needed, and allow others to express their feelings and experiences without judgment.
2. **Flexibility at Work:**
   o **Principle:** Many companies have adopted remote working during the pandemic, and this trend will continue in 2024.
   o **Action:** Negotiate flexible work arrangements with employers, balance work from home and in the office, and create a healthy workspace at home.
3. **Prioritizing Well-being:**
   o **Principle:** The pandemic has highlighted the importance of health and well-being.

o   **Action:** Integrate self-care routines, such as meditation, physical exercise, and a balanced diet. Take regular breaks and disconnect from screens.

4.   **Networking and Social Connection:**
   o   **Principle:** Pandemic restrictions have limited social interactions, but in 2024, it's time to reconnect with community.
   o   **Action:** Attend local events, join interest groups or clubs, and use technology to stay connected with distant family and friends.

5.   **Continuing Education:**
   o   **Principle:** The post-pandemic world is constantly changing, and continuous learning is essential.
   o   **Action:** Take online courses, attend workshops or seminars, and stay informed about the latest trends and innovations.

6.   **Responsible Travel:**
   o   **Principle:** As travel resumes, it is crucial to do so responsibly and consciously.
   o   **Action:** Learn about health and safety guidelines, choose eco-responsible destinations, and respect local cultures and communities.

Conclusion:

The year 2024 will be a time of reflection, adaptation and growth. By recognizing the challenges and lessons learned during the pandemic, we can move forward with resilience, compassion and hope. Adapting to the new normal requires a proactive approach, focused on individual and collective well-being.

4.2.2 Emerging Technologies for Well-being

As we enter 2024, technology continues to play a leading role in how we approach and understand well-being. Here are some of the emerging technologies shaping the wellness landscape:

1. **Meditation and Mindfulness Applications:**
    o **Principle:** These apps use guided techniques to help users refocus, reduce stress and improve concentration.
    o **Action:** Incorporate daily meditation sessions using popular apps to improve mental health.

2. **Smart Clothing:**
    o **Principle:** Clothing equipped with sensors that monitor vital signs, posture and even mood.
    o **Action:** Use these clothes to get real-time feedback on physical and emotional health, and adjust routines accordingly.

3. **Virtual Reality (VR) for Therapy:**
    o **Principle:** VR provides immersive experiences to treat problems such as post-traumatic stress, anxiety and phobia.
    o **Action:** Participate in VR therapy sessions to address specific issues in a controlled environment.

4. **Connected Fitness Platforms:**
   o **Principle:** These platforms offer live classes, performance tracking and communities to encourage physical activity.
   o **Action:** Incorporate regular workouts using these platforms to stay active and motivated.
5. **Biofeedback and Neurofeedback:**
   o **Principle:** These technologies allow users to receive real-time information on their body and brain functions.
   o **Action:** Use biofeedback to understand how the body reacts to stress and learn to regulate these responses.
6. **Intelligent Sleep Assistants:**
   o **Principle:** Devices that monitor sleep cycles, sleep quality and provide recommendations to improve rest.
   o **Action:** Integrate these technologies into the nighttime routine to optimize sleep.
7. **Personalized Nutrition Applications:**
   o **Principle:** These apps provide dietary recommendations based on genetics, microbiome and personal preferences.
   o **Action:** Use these apps to create a diet tailored to individual needs.

Conclusion:

In 2024, technology and well-being will be inextricably linked. Technological innovations offer valuable tools to improve physical, mental and emotional health. By adopting these emerging technologies, we can take proactive steps to improve our well-being and live more balanced and fulfilling lives.

4.2.3 Eco-responsibility and Well-being

The year 2024 will mark increased awareness of the interconnection between eco-responsibility and individual well-being. Here is how this relationship will manifest itself and how it will influence our approach to well-being:

1. **Environmental Awareness and Mental Health:**
   o **Principle:** Environmental degradation, such as air pollution and loss of biodiversity, has adverse effects on mental health. Conversely, a healthy environment promotes well-being.
   o **Action:** Engage in reforestation activities, beach cleanups and other eco-friendly initiatives to improve the environment and, therefore, mental well-being.
2. **Sustainable Food:**
   o **Principle:** A diet based on local, organic and seasonal products not only promotes physical health, but also reduces the carbon footprint.
   o **Action:** Favor local markets, reduce meat consumption and avoid over-packaged

products to support a sustainable diet.

3. **Minimalist Lifestyle:**
   o **Principle:** Living with less reduces overconsumption, reduces stress and promotes a more centered and balanced life.
   o **Action:** Adopt decluttering practices, reduce impulse purchases and value experiences over material possessions.

4. **Ecological Transport:**
   o **Principle:** Opting for ecological means of transport reduces the carbon footprint and promotes physical health.
   o **Action:** Favor walking, cycling, public transport or electric vehicles for daily travel.

5. **Relaxation practices in the great outdoors:**
   o **Principle:** Nature has a calming effect on the mind and body. Outdoor relaxation practices, such as forest therapy or nature meditation, strengthen this connection.
   o **Action:** Integrate outdoor relaxation sessions into the daily routine to benefit from the therapeutic benefits of nature.

6. **Responsible Consumption:**
   o **Principle:** Buying ethical and sustainable products not only supports the environment, but also reinforces a sense of accomplishment and responsibility.
   o **Action:** Look for eco-friendly certifications when purchasing products and support ethical businesses.

Conclusion:

Eco-responsibility is not just a trend, it is a necessity for the well-being of our planet and its inhabitants. In 2024, awareness of the importance of living eco-responsibly will be greater than ever. By adopting eco-friendly practices in our daily lives, we will not only contribute to the health of our planet, but also to our own well-being.

4.2.4 Food Trends of 2024

The year 2024 will see the emergence of new food trends, influenced by environmental, technological, cultural and health concerns. Here's a look at the top trends that will dominate the culinary landscape:

1. **Plant-Based Foods:**
   - **Principle:** With increasing awareness of the environmental and health impacts of meat consumption, plant-based foods have become a popular alternative.
   - **Action:** Increased consumption of plant-based meat alternatives, such as vegan burgers, meat-free sausages and dairy alternatives.
2. **Fermentation and Probiotics:**
   - **Principle:** Gut health has become a major concern, leading to an increase in the consumption of fermented foods rich in probiotics.
   - **Action:** Growing popularity of kombucha, kimchi, miso and plant-based yogurt.

3. **Adaptogenic Foods:**
   o **Principle:** Adaptogens are herbs and mushrooms that help the body resist physical and mental stress.
   o **Action:** Incorporation of ingredients such as ginseng, ashwagandha root and reishi into smoothies, teas and other preparations.
4. **Zero Waste Kitchen:**
   o **Principle:** In an eco-responsible approach, the trend is to reduce food waste.
   o **Action:** Use of all parts of a food, organization of zero waste cooking workshops and promotion of composting.
5. **Technology and Food:**
   o **Principle:** Technological innovation influences the way we produce, consume and understand food.
   o **Action:** Increased use of nutritional tracking apps, 3D printed food production, and drone meal delivery.
6. **Local Superfoods:**
   o **Principle:** Instead of searching for exotic superfoods, the emphasis is on rediscovering local, nutritious foods.
   o **Action:** Promotion of local berries, seeds and vegetables as sources of antioxidants, vitamins and minerals.
7. **Ethnic Fusion Cuisine:**
   o **Principle:** The fusion of different world cuisines creates innovative and delicious

dishes.

- o **Action:** Emergence of restaurants and recipes combining elements of different culinary traditions.

Conclusion:

The food trends of 2024 will reflect a shift towards more conscious, sustainable and innovative eating. Consumers are increasingly informed and concerned about the origin of their food and its impact on health and the environment. These trends show a desire to combine taste pleasure, well-being and ethical responsibility.

4.2.5 Innovative Living and Working Spaces

As we enter 2024, the way we perceive and use our living and working spaces has undergone radical transformations. These changes are the result of a combination of technological, environmental and socio-cultural factors. Here is an overview of the major trends shaping our spaces at the end of the year:

1. **Flexible Offices:**
   - o **Principle:** With the rise of teleworking, companies are adopting modular office spaces that can be adapted according to needs.
   - o **Action:** Versatile coworking spaces, modular meeting rooms and relaxation zones to encourage creativity and collaboration.

2. **Sustainable Habitats:**
   o **Principle:** Faced with the climate crisis, the design of environmentally friendly habitats has become a priority.
   o **Action:** Use of recycled materials, integration of energy saving technologies and bioclimatic design for better energy efficiency.
3. **Integrated Technology:**
   o **Principle:** Technology has become an integral part of our living and working spaces.
   o **Action:** Smart homes and offices equipped with automation systems, augmented reality and IoT devices to improve comfort and efficiency.
4. **Integrated Green Spaces:**
   o **Principle:** Nature is integrated into the design of spaces to improve well-being and air quality.
   o **Action:** Vertical gardens, green roofs and outdoor relaxation spaces in urban areas.
5. **Multifunctional Areas:**
   o **Principle:** Spaces are designed to be versatile in order to maximize their utility.
   o **Action:** Rooms that can be used as an office, gym or guest bedroom, depending on needs.
6. **Connected Communities:**
   o **Principle:** Residential and work spaces are designed to foster community and human

connection.

- o **Action:** Shared common spaces, neighborhood apps and community events to strengthen social connections.

7. **Well-Being-Focused Design:**
   - o **Principle:** Spaces are designed with well-being in mind, emphasizing natural light, fresh air and calming elements.
   - o **Action:** Use of calming colors, integration of nature and optimization of light and ventilation.

Conclusion:

In 2024, the spaces in which we live and work will no longer just be functional places, but environments designed to improve our quality of life, our well-being and our productivity. These innovations reflect a growing awareness of the importance of the environment in our mental and physical health, as well as the need to adopt sustainable practices for the future of our planet.

4.2.6 Virtual Communities and Networking

As technology advances and the world becomes more interconnected, virtual communities and online networking are becoming increasingly important in people's lives. Here is an overview of this trend for 2024:

1. **Emergence of the Metaverses:**
   - o **Principle:** Metaverses, or persistent virtual

universes, have become spaces where people can interact, work, play and even do business.

- o **Action:** Platforms like Facebook Horizon and Decentraland offer immersive experiences, allowing users to create avatars, purchase virtual land and interact in a digital world.

2. **Virtual Professional Networking:**

- o **Principle:** Professional events, conferences and workshops are increasingly moving online, providing networking opportunities on a global scale.
- o **Action:** Platforms like Hopin and Zoom organize virtual events where participants can attend sessions, visit booths and interact with other professionals.

3. **Niche Communities:**

- o **Principle:** Online platforms enable the formation of communities around specific interests, ranging from hobbies to professions.
- o **Action:** Sites like Reddit, Discord, and Clubhouse provide spaces where individuals can share knowledge, ask questions, and build relationships.

4. **Online Training and Education:**

- o **Principle:** Online learning platforms provide education and training opportunities for those looking to learn new skills.
- o **Action:** Platforms like Coursera, Udemy, and Khan Academy offer courses on a variety of

topics, allowing users to learn at their own pace.

5. **Support and Well-being:**
   o **Principle:** Virtual communities provide emotional and mental support to those who need it, especially during these uncertain times.
   o **Action:** Online support groups, virtual therapy sessions, and meditation apps like Headspace and Calm help individuals manage stress and anxiety.
6. **Diversity and Inclusion:**
   o **Principle:** Online communities provide a space where diversity is celebrated and marginalized voices can be heard.
   o **Action:** Dedicated forums and groups provide support and a platform for minorities, LGBTQ+ and other underrepresented groups.

Conclusion:

In 2024, virtual communities and online networking will not just be complements to our physical interactions, but essential elements of our social and professional lives. They offer unprecedented opportunities for learning, growth and connection, breaking down geographical and cultural barriers.

4.2.7 Social Movements and Well-being

The year 2024 will see a convergence between social movements and the quest for individual and collective well-being. Here is how these movements will influence and shape the perception and practice of well-being:

1. **Egalitarian Well-being:**
   - **Principle:** The recognition that well-being should not be a luxury reserved for a few, but a right for all.
   - **Action:** Initiatives to make mental health care, therapies and wellness resources accessible to everyone, regardless of socioeconomic status.

2. **Climate Justice Movement:**
   - **Principle:** The awareness that the health of our planet is intrinsically linked to our individual well-being.
   - **Action:** Sustainable wellness practices, such as outdoor yoga, nature meditation, and adopting eco-friendly diets.

3. **Feminism and Well-being:**
   - **Principle:** The importance of recognizing and responding to the specific well-being needs of women.
   - **Action:** Programs and resources focused on women's well-being, addressing topics like reproductive health, dual burden stress, and empowerment through movement.

4. **Anti-discrimination movements:**
   - **Principle:** Combating discrimination based

on race, sexuality, gender and other identities.

- o **Action:** Inclusive wellness spaces that celebrate diversity and offer specific support to marginalized groups.

5. **Well-being and Activism:**
   - o **Principle:** The understanding that activism can be emotionally and mentally draining, requiring wellness practices to support activists.
   - o **Action:** Workshops and resources dedicated to helping activists manage stress, fatigue and burnout.

6. **Responsible Technology:**
   - o **Principle:** The idea that technology should be designed and used in a way that supports the well-being of users.
   - o **Action:** The emergence of apps and platforms that encourage digital breaks, mindfulness and regular disconnection.

Conclusion:

In 2024, well-being will no longer be seen as an isolated individual quest, but as an aspiration deeply rooted in the social fabric. Social movements have played a crucial role in redefining what well-being means, placing it in a broader context of equity, justice and collective responsibility.

4.2.8 Travel and Well-

being Experiences

As we enter 2024, the concept of travel has evolved far beyond simply exploring new destinations. Travel has become a quest for well-being, an opportunity to reconnect with yourself, with nature and with different cultures. Here's how travel and wellness experiences showed up this year:

1. **Wellness Retreats:**
    o **Principle:** Getaways to remote destinations, focused on meditation, yoga, detoxification and spiritual healing.
    o **Action:** Retreat centers offering comprehensive programs, from Ayurvedic treatments in India to thermal baths in Iceland.

2. **Ecological Tourism:**
    o **Principle:** Travel responsibly, minimizing the ecological footprint and immersing yourself in nature.
    o **Action:** Stays in eco-lodges, hikes in nature reserves and sustainable camping experiences.

3. **Holistic Cultural Trips:**
    o **Principle:** Discover ancestral traditions of well-being in different cultures.
    o **Action:** Participate in traditional ceremonies, learn local healing practices, and enjoy healthy regional cuisines.

4. **Detached Digital Travel:**

o **Principle:** Take a break from omnipresent technologies to disconnect and refocus.

o **Action:** Destinations without Wi-Fi, digital detox workshops and stays without electronic devices.

5. **Urban Well-being Experiences:**

o **Principle:** Find serenity and well-being in the heart of bustling metropolises.

o **Action:** Urban meditation studios, wellness parks and spas on city rooftops.

6. **Transformation Journeys:**

o **Principle:** Journeys designed to provoke profound inner change.

o **Action:** Personalized itineraries focused on personal growth, self-discovery and emotional healing.

Conclusion:

In 2024, travel will no longer just be an escape, but a deep immersion in experiences that nourish the soul, body and spirit. Individuals will seek authentic experiences that help them reconnect, revitalize and find meaning in an ever-changing world. Wellness travel meets this need, offering a unique fusion of relaxation, adventure and self-discovery.

4.2.9 Education and Continuous Learning

The year 2024 will mark a significant transformation in the way we view education and learning. In an ever-changing world marked by rapid technological advancements and social upheaval, education is no longer limited to the traditional classroom. Here's how education and lifelong learning showed up this year:

1. **Lifelong Learning:**
   o **Principle:** Recognize that learning is a lifelong journey that does not end with a degree or certificate.
   o **Action:** Flexible study programs, online courses and workshops that encourage individuals to continue learning at every stage of their lives.
2. **Educational Technologies:**
   o **Principle:** Use technology to enhance the educational experience.
   o **Action:** Interactive learning platforms, virtual reality for immersive learning experiences and self-learning applications.
3. **Holistic Education:**
   o **Principle:** Integrate mental, emotional and physical well-being into the educational curriculum.
   o **Action:** Courses on mindfulness, stress management and emotional intelligence integrated into school curricula.
4. **Experiential Learning:**
   o **Principle:** Learn through direct experience rather than simple memorization.
   o **Action:** Internships, educational trips and

hands-on projects that provide a hands-on learning experience.

5.   **Learning Communities:**
   o   **Principle:** Create spaces where people can learn together, share knowledge and collaborate.
   o   **Action:** Online study groups, discussion forums and community workshops.

6.   **Personalized Education:**
   o **Principle:** Recognize that each individual has unique needs and learning styles.
   o   **Action:** Adapted learning paths, personalized assessments and tailor-made educational resources.

Conclusion:

In 2024, education has become a dynamic and adaptive process, focused on the holistic development of the individual. The emphasis is on developing practical skills, emotional resilience and the ability to adapt to a constantly changing world. Continuous learning is not only encouraged, but also considered essential to successfully navigate the challenges of the 21st century.

4.2.10 Information Management and Disinformation

In the era of digitalization and globalization, 2024 has seen an unprecedented explosion of information. While this has allowed unprecedented access to knowledge, it has also led to an increase in misinformation. Here is how modern society approaches this challenge:

1. **Media Literacy Education:**
    o **Principle:** Equip individuals with the skills to assess the credibility of information sources.
    o **Action:** Integration of media literacy courses into school programs, adult workshops and awareness campaigns.
2. **Responsible Platforms:**
    o **Principle:** Social media platforms and search engines have the responsibility to regulate and filter content.
    o **Action:** Using advanced algorithms to detect and report misinformation, implementing fact checkers and trust labels.
3. **Public Awareness:**
    o **Principle:** Inform the general public of the dangers of misinformation and how to recognize it.
    o **Action:** Advertising campaigns, documentaries, and community initiatives.
4. **International collaboration:**
    o **Principle:** Disinformation is a global problem requiring a coordinated response.
    o **Action:** International agreements, conferences and collaborations between countries to combat the spread of false information.

5. **Transparency of Sources:**
   - o **Principle:** Information sources must be transparent about their affiliations, funding and intentions.
   - o **Action:** Legislation requiring full disclosure of media funding sources, transparency labels on articles and publications.
6. **Critical Education:**
   - o **Principle:** Encourage critical thinking among information consumers.
   - o **Action:** Educational programs that teach how to ask questions, research multiple sources, and avoid confirmation bias.

Conclusion:

In 2024, in the face of the rising tide of misinformation, society will take proactive steps to ensure that individuals are well-informed and equipped to distinguish fact from error. Managing information and misinformation will become an essential skill, just as important as traditional literacy, and will be seen as a pillar of responsible citizenship.

CHAPTER 5: PERSONALIZED ACTION PLAN

"Rest and recovery are essential to avoiding burnout; they are not a sign of weakness."

Karen A. Baar

5.1 How to create an action plan

5.1.1 Personal Assessment

Personal assessment is the crucial first step in creating an effective action plan against burnout. It helps identify specific areas of one's life that require attention and intervention. Here's how to do it:

1. **Self-reflection:**
   o **Principle:** Take a moment for yourself, in a calm environment, to reflect on your current state.

o **Action:** Keep a journal, writing down your feelings, thoughts, worries and hopes.

2.   **Questionnaires and Tests:**
   o **Principle:** Use validated tools to assess your level of stress, anxiety, depression and exhaustion.
   o **Action:** Complete questionnaires such as the Maslach Burnout Inventory or mental health assessment tests.

3.   **Identify Triggers:**
   o **Principle:** Recognize the specific factors that contribute to your feeling of burnout.
   o **Action:** Make a list of professional and personal stresses, unrealistic expectations, relationship conflicts, etc.

4.   **Assess your Needs:**
   o **Principle:** Understand what we need to feel balanced and satisfied.
   o **Action:** Identify unmet needs for sleep, nutrition, free time, social connection, etc.

5.   **Recognize your Strengths and Weaknesses:**
   o **Principle:** Accept your limits while recognizing your skills.
   o **Action:** Take an inventory of your talents, skills, passions and areas for improvement.

6.   **Feedback from loved ones:**
   o **Principle:** Obtain outside perspectives to see the big picture.
   o **Action:** Ask friends, family or colleagues to

share their observations about his behavior and well-being.

Conclusion:

Personal evaluation is an introspective step that requires honesty and vulnerability. It lays the foundation for an action plan by providing a clear understanding of where one is currently and the areas that require intervention. With this information in hand, we can develop targeted strategies to overcome burnout and regain balance in our lives.

5.1.2 Definition of Clear Objectives

Defining clear objectives is an essential step in guiding your path to healing and preventing burnout. It provides clear direction and measurable steps to progress toward optimal well-being. Here's how to set clear, achievable goals:

1. **Specificity:**
   o **Principle:** A well-defined objective is a specific objective. Avoid generalizations.
   o **Action:** Instead of saying "I want to be less stressed," opt for "I'm going to meditate for 10 minutes every morning."
2. **Measurability:**
   o **Principle:** To know if you are progressing, your objective must be quantifiable.
   o **Action:** "I will walk 30 minutes a day" rather than "I will walk more".
3. **Achievability:**
   o **Principle:** Set realistic goals based on your

current capabilities and resources.

- o **Action:** If you've never run, don't aim for a marathon in a month. Start with shorter runs.

4. **Relevance:**
   - o **Principle:** Your goals should be aligned with your values and long-term aspirations.
   - o **Action:** If health is a priority, an objective linked to a balanced diet would be relevant.

5. **Temporality:**
   - o **Principle:** Every goal should have a deadline to create a sense of urgency and motivation.
   - o **Action:** "I'm going to read a book on stress management by the end of the month."

6. **Revision and Adjustment:**
   - o **Principle:** Circumstances change, and it is essential to review and adjust your goals accordingly.
   - o **Action:** If an injury prevents you from running, adapt your goal to another form of exercise.

7. **Visualization:**
   - o **Principle:** Clearly imagining achieving your goals can strengthen your commitment to them.
   - o **Action:** Take a few minutes each day to visualize your success.

Bottom line:

Setting clear goals is like drawing a map for your journey to wellness. It gives you direction, steps to follow, and a way to measure your progress. By staying committed and adjusting your goals as needed, you give yourself the best chance of overcoming burnout and living a balanced, fulfilling life.

5.1.3 Daily Planning

Daily planning is a powerful tool for managing your time, energies and priorities. It allows you to structure your day, focus on the essentials and avoid the feeling of being overwhelmed. Here's how to develop an effective daily plan to promote well-being and prevent burnout:

1. **Start the Day with Intention:**
   - **Principle:** Start each day with a clear vision of what you want to accomplish.
   - **Action:** Take 5 minutes each morning to define your top three priorities for the day.
2. **Time Blocking:**
   - **Principle:** Allocate specific blocks of time for each task or activity.
   - **Action:** If you have a meeting from 10 a.m. to 11 a.m., block this slot in your calendar.
3. **Strategic Breaks:**
   - **Principle:** Include regular breaks to recharge your batteries and avoid fatigue.
   - **Action:** Every 90 minutes, take a 10-minute break to stretch, breathe or walk.
4. **Avoid Multitasking:**
   - **Principle:** Multitasking can reduce the

quality of work and increase stress.

- o **Action:** Focus on one task at a time and avoid distractions.

5. **End of Day Review:**
- o **Principle:** Take a moment at the end of the day to evaluate what you have accomplished and prepare for the next day.
- o **Action:** List what you accomplished and identify tasks for the next day.

6. **Prioritization:**
- o **Principle:** Not all tasks are of equal importance. Focus on what really matters.
- o **Action:** Use the Eisenhower method to rank tasks based on urgency and importance.

7. **Flexibility:**
- o **Principle:** While planning is essential, remaining adaptable is equally crucial.
- o **Action:** If an emergency arises, readjust your planning without guilt.

8. **Space for yourself:**
- o **Principle:** Set aside time each day for activities that nourish you mentally, emotionally, and physically.
- o **Action:** Whether it's meditation, reading, or going for a walk, make sure you have some time to yourself.

Bottom line:

Daily planning is more than just a to-do list. It's a holistic approach to managing your day with intention and awareness. By integrating these principles, you can create a daily routine that supports your well-being, builds your resilience, and moves you back from the brink of burnout.

5.1.4 Stress Management Strategies

Stress is our body's natural response to the challenges and pressures of daily life. However, prolonged exposure to stress can lead to burnout and other health problems. It is therefore essential to have effective strategies to manage stress. Here are some proven methods to achieve this:

1. **Deep Breathing:**
   o **Principle:** Deep breathing activates the parasympathetic nervous system, which helps calm the body and mind.
   o **Action:** Take a few minutes each day to practice abdominal breathing, inhaling deeply through your nose and exhaling slowly through your mouth.
2. **Regular Exercise:**
   o **Principle:** Physical activity releases endorphins, neurotransmitters that act as natural painkillers.
   o **Action:** Integrate a daily exercise routine, whether it's walking, yoga, swimming, or any other sport you enjoy.
3. **Meditation and Mindfulness:**
   o **Principle:** Meditation helps refocus the mind and reduce anxiety.
   o **Action:** Spend a few minutes each day meditating or practicing mindfulness.

4.   **Establish Boundaries:**
   o **Principle:** It is crucial to know how to say no and define clear limits to avoid overwork.
   o **Action:** Evaluate your commitments and learn to politely decline requests that don't align with your priorities.
5.   **Break time :**
   o **Principle:** Everyone needs time to relax and recharge.
   o **Action:** Set aside time each week for activities you enjoy, whether that's reading, listening to music, or gardening.
6.   **Balanced diet :**
   o **Principle:** A healthy diet supports cognitive function and regulates energy levels.
   o **Action:** Eat balanced meals with a variety of nutritious foods and avoid excess caffeine and sugar.
7.   **Sufficient Sleep:**
   o **Principle:** Sleep is essential for mental and physical recovery.
   o **Action:** Aim for 7 to 9 hours of sleep per night and maintain a regular sleep routine.
8.   **Social Connection:**
   o **Principle:** Social interactions can provide emotional support and reduce feelings of isolation.
   o **Action:** Spend time with friends and family, or consider joining a support group.
9.   **Artistic Practices:**

o   **Principle:** Creative activities can be therapeutic and provide an escape from everyday stress.

o **Action:** Try painting, writing, dancing, or any other art that excites you.

10.   **Avoid Excessive Consumption of Alcohol and Drugs:**

o   **Principle:** Although some people use alcohol and drugs as a way to escape stress, it can make the problem worse in the long run.

o   **Action:** If you choose to consume, do so in moderation.

Conclusion:

Stress management is an essential skill in the modern world. By integrating these strategies into your daily life, you can not only effectively manage stress, but also improve your overall quality of life and prevent burnout.

5.1.5 Establishing Boundaries

Setting boundaries is an essential skill for maintaining a healthy balance between work, play and personal relationships. Boundaries help us define what we are willing to accept and what we will not tolerate, both in our professional and personal lives. Here's how and why setting boundaries is crucial:

1. **Understand the Importance of Boundaries:**

o **Principle:** Boundaries protect our emotional, mental, and physical well-being. They allow us to distinguish our needs, desires and rights from others.

o **Action:** Take the time to think about your values and what is essential to you.

2. **Identify your Limits:**

o **Principle:** Everyone has their own limits based on their experiences, culture, personality and values.

o **Action:** Evaluate situations where you felt uncomfortable or overwhelmed and identify boundaries that were crossed.

3. **Communicate Clearly:**

o **Principle:** It is essential to express your limits clearly and assertively.

o **Action:** Practice assertive communication techniques to express your needs without being aggressive or passive.

4. **Learn to Say No:**

o **Principle:** Saying no is a powerful way to set boundaries.

o **Action:** If something doesn't suit you or doesn't align with your values, have the courage to politely decline.

5. **Avoid Work Overload:**

o **Principle:** Taking on too many commitments can lead to burnout.

o **Action:** Regularly assess your workload and delegate or decline tasks as necessary.

6. **Protecting Your Personal Time:**

o **Principle:** Personal time is essential to

recharge and relax.

- o **Action:** Block specific periods in your schedule for activities you enjoy.

7. **Recognize Warning Signals:**
   - o **Principle:** Your body and mind will send you signals when your limits are crossed.
   - o **Action:** Pay attention to signs of stress, anxiety or fatigue and adjust your limits accordingly.

8. **Review and Adjust:**
   - o **Principle:** Boundaries can evolve over time as circumstances or perspectives change.
   - o **Action:** Reassess your limits regularly and make adjustments as necessary.

Bottom line:

Setting boundaries is an act of empowerment. This empowers you to take control of your life, protect your well-being, and build healthy, respectful relationships. By understanding your own limitations and communicating them effectively to others, you create an environment where you can thrive and flourish.

5.1.6 Support and Resources

Support and resources are essential elements in overcoming burnout and putting an effective action plan in place. They provide a solid foundation for healing, growth and personal development. Here's how to maximize the use of available support and resources:

1. **Recognize the Need for Support:**

- o **Principle:** No one is an island. We all need support at different times in our lives, especially during difficult times.
- o **Action:** Accept that asking for help is a sign of strength, not weakness.

2. **Professional Support:**
- o **Principle:** Therapists, counselors and coaches can offer valuable perspectives and tools for managing stress and burnout.
- o **Action:** Consider consulting a professional for advice and strategies tailored to your situation.

3. **Social Support Networks:**
- o **Principle:** Friends, family and colleagues can offer emotional support, practical advice and a listening ear.
- o **Action:** Share your feelings and concerns with people you trust and attend support groups or workshops.

4. **Online Resources:**
- o **Principle:** Many websites, applications and forums offer information, tools and communities to help manage burnout.
- o **Action:** Find reliable resources online and use wellness or meditation apps.

5. **Training and Workshops:**
- o **Principle:** Workshops and training can provide skills and techniques to manage stress, improve resilience and promote well-being.

o **Action:** Sign up for workshops or courses that match your needs and interests.
6.   **Literature and Media:**
   o **Principle:** Books, podcasts and videos can offer perspectives, stories and strategies for overcoming burnout.
   o **Action:** Explore literature and media on wellness, stress management, and healing from burnout.
7.   **Community Events:**
   o **Principle:** Participating in local events can provide a sense of belonging and an opportunity to connect with others with similar experiences.
   o **Action:** Look for local events or groups focused on wellness and mental health.
8.   **Establish a Support Network:**
   o **Principle:** Having a strong support network can make a big difference in how you manage and overcome burnout.
   o **Action:** Identify people around you who can support you and establish regular connections with them.

Bottom Line:

The path to healing from burnout is often a journey that requires both internal and external support. By recognizing the value of support and actively using available resources, you can create an environment conducive to healing, growth and lasting well-being.

5.1.7 Monitoring and Reassessment

Monitoring and reassessment are crucial steps in any action plan to overcome burnout. They help ensure that the strategies put in place are effective and offer the opportunity to make adjustments based on changes in life and individual needs. Here's how to approach these steps:

1. **Importance of Monitoring:**
   o **Principle:** Just as a doctor monitors the progress of a disease, it is essential to regularly monitor your progress to ensure that you are moving in the right direction.
   o **Action:** Set up regular reminders to assess your emotional, physical and mental state.
2. **Logbook :**
   o **Principle:** Keeping a journal of your feelings, activities, and reactions can help you identify specific trends or triggers.
   o **Action:** Spend a few minutes each day writing down your experiences, emotions, and thoughts.
3. **Reassessment of the Objectives:**
   o **Principle:** Needs and circumstances can change over time. It is therefore essential to re-evaluate your goals regularly to ensure they remain relevant.
   o **Action:** Review your goals monthly to see if they are still aligned with your current aspirations.

4. **Feedback from loved ones:**
   o **Principle:** Friends, family, and colleagues can offer valuable perspectives on your progress and well-being.
   o **Action:** Ask your loved ones regularly for feedback on the changes they observe in you.

5. **Necessary Adjustments:**
   o **Principle:** If something is not working as expected, it is crucial to be flexible and make adjustments as necessary.
   o **Action:** If a particular strategy does not produce the expected results, explore other options or approaches.

6. **Celebrating Achievements:**
   o **Principle:** Recognizing and celebrating small victories can build motivation and a sense of accomplishment.
   o **Action:** Take time to celebrate your progress, whether big or small.

7. **Planning of Regular Reviews:**
   o **Principle:** Setting specific dates to review your action plan can help maintain accountability and commitment.
   o **Action:** Schedule quarterly reviews to assess your progress and adjust your plan accordingly.

Bottom line:

The process of healing from burnout is a journey, not a destination. Regular monitoring and reassessment ensures that you stay on track, adapting to changes and challenges while celebrating your successes along the way. These steps keep you engaged, motivated, and focused on your overall well-being.

5.1.8 Integration of Well-being Practices

Integrating wellness practices into daily life is essential to preventing and healing from burnout. These practices can help build resilience, improve mental and physical health, and create balance in life. Here's how to effectively integrate these practices:

1. **Needs Assessment:**
   o **Principle:** Before incorporating wellness practices, it is crucial to assess your personal needs and what resonates most with you.
   o **Action:** Think about what brings you the most peace, joy and relaxation. This may vary from person to person.
2. **Daily routine :**
   o **Principle:** Regularity is the key. Integrate wellness practices into your daily routine to reap the maximum benefits.
   o **Action:** Set aside time each day, even if it's just a few minutes, for an activity that promotes your well-being, such as meditation, reading or exercising.

3.   **Training and Learning:**
   o **Principle:** It is essential to understand and master the techniques to get the most out of them.
   o   **Action:** Consider taking classes or workshops on specific wellness practices that interest you.
4.   **Dedicated area :**
   o   **Principle:** Having a dedicated space for practicing well-being can strengthen engagement and improve the experience.
   o **Action:** Create a peaceful corner in your home for meditation, yoga or any other relaxation practice.
5.   **Community and Support:**
   o **Principle:** Being surrounded by like-minded people can boost motivation and provide valuable support.
   o **Action:** Join wellness-focused groups or communities, whether online or locally.
6.   **Evolution and Adaptation:**
   o   **Principle:** Needs and preferences may change over time. Be open to exploration and adaptation.
   o **Action:** Try different wellness practices and see what works best for you at different times in your life.
7.   **Measuring Progress:**
   o   **Principle:** Tracking your progress can help you stay motivated and recognize the

benefits of wellness practices.

- o **Action:** Keep a wellness journal to record your feelings, your progress, and the changes you observe.

Conclusion:

Integrating wellness practices requires commitment and intentionality. By being aware of your needs, establishing routines and seeking support, you can make wellbeing an integral part of your life, promoting better health, balance and resilience in the face of challenges.

5.1.9 Management of Unforeseen Events

Life is unpredictable, and even with a well-structured action plan, unexpected events can occur. The ability to manage these unexpected events is crucial to maintaining well-being and avoiding burnout. Here are some strategies for effectively navigating through the unexpected:

1. **Acceptance and Letting Go:**
   - o **Principle:** Recognizing that some things are beyond our control is the first step in managing the unexpected.
   - o **Action:** Instead of resisting or denying the situation, accept it as it is and focus on what you can control.
2. **Deep breathing :**
   - o **Principle:** Deep breathing can help calm the mind and reduce stress instantly.

o   **Action:** When faced with something unexpected, take a moment to breathe deeply, this will help you respond more thoughtfully.

3.   **Quick Assessment:**
   o **Principle:** Quickly assess the situation to determine the best way to respond.
   o **Action:** Ask yourself questions like: "What is the priority here?" or "What is the best action to take now?"

4.   **Plan B :**
   o **Principle:** Having a backup plan for common situations can help reduce anxiety about the unknown.
   o **Action:** Think about possible scenarios and how you might respond to them.

5.   **Looking for Support:**
   o **Principle:** Sharing your concerns or asking for help can ease the burden of the unexpected.
   o **Action:** Talk to a trusted friend, colleague, or professional for advice or just to vent.

6.   **Flexibility:**
   o   **Principle:** Being flexible allows you to quickly adapt your plans according to changing circumstances.
   o **Action:** Cultivate an open mindset and be willing to adjust your plans if necessary.

7.   **Mental Preparation:**
   o **Principle:** Train your mind to anticipate

challenges and develop resilience in the face of adversity.

- o **Action:** Practice meditation, visualization, or other mental strengthening techniques.

8. **Review and Learning:**

- o **Principle:** Every unexpected event is an opportunity to learn and grow.
- o **Action:** After handling an unexpected situation, take a moment to reflect on what went well, what could have been done differently, and what you can learn for the future.

Conclusion:

Managing the unexpected is an essential skill in modern life. By taking a proactive approach, remaining flexible, and learning from each experience, you can successfully navigate unexpected challenges and maintain your well-being.

5.1.10 Celebrating Achievements

Recognizing and celebrating your successes is an essential element of well-being and burnout prevention. This not only helps build self-confidence, but also recognizes progress made. Here's how and why it's important to celebrate your successes:

1. **Recognition of Effort:**

- o **Principle:** Every milestone achieved, no matter how small, is the result of effort and dedication.

o **Action:** Take a moment to recognize the effort you have invested to achieve your goals.

2. **Strengthening Self-Confidence:**
   o **Principle:** Celebrating your successes builds your confidence in your ability to achieve your goals.
   o **Action:** Regularly remind yourself of your past achievements to boost your self-confidence.

3. **Increased Motivation:**
   o **Principle:** Celebrating successes can serve as motivation to achieve even greater goals.
   o **Action:** Use your successes as a springboard to set even more ambitious goals.

4. **Recognition of Progress:**
   o **Principle:** It is essential to recognize progress made, even if it is small.
   o **Action:** Keep a journal of your successes or create a vision board to visualize your progress.

5. **Sharing Joy:**
   o **Principle:** Sharing your successes with others can multiply joy and a sense of accomplishment.
   o **Action:** Share your moments of success with friends, family or colleagues to celebrate together.

6. **Personal Reward:**
   o **Principle:** Rewarding yourself for success

reinforces the feeling of accomplishment.

o **Action:** Treat yourself to something you like or do an activity you enjoy as a reward.

7. **Reflection and Gratitude:**

o **Principle:** Take a moment to reflect on what you have accomplished and express gratitude for the opportunities and support received.

o **Action:** Practice gratitude regularly by recognizing the people and circumstances that have contributed to your successes.

8. **Planning Next Steps:**

o **Principle:** After celebrating an achievement, it is beneficial to think about next steps.

o **Action:** Use the moment of celebration as an opportunity to plan your next goals.

Conclusion:

Celebrating your successes is not an act of arrogance, but rather a recognition of effort, dedication and perseverance. It's an essential way to recharge your batteries, motivate yourself, and continue moving toward even bigger goals.

5.2 Resources and support available

5.2.1 Mental Health Professionals

Mental health is just as crucial as physical health. In the context of burnout, it is essential to recognize when you need help and know where to turn. Mental health professionals play a key role in the prevention, diagnosis and treatment of burnout.

1. **Psychologists:**
   - **Description:** Psychologists are trained to understand and treat behavioral, emotional and mental problems. They use a variety of therapeutic techniques to help individuals manage their symptoms.
   - **When to see them:** If you experience persistent emotional distress, negative thoughts, or difficulty managing stress.
2. **Psychiatrists:**
   - **Description:** Psychiatrists are doctors specializing in the diagnosis, treatment and prevention of mental disorders. They can prescribe medications and offer therapies.
   - **When to see them:** If your symptoms are severe or if you think you need medical evaluation or medication.
3. **Counselors and therapists:**
   - **Description:** These professionals offer counseling and therapy for a variety of issues, including stress, anxiety and depression.
   - **When to see them:** If you feel the need to talk about your problems, feelings or concerns.
4. **Life and well-being coaches:**
   - **Description:** They focus on

personal development, achieving goals and improving overall well-being.

- o **When to check them out:** If you're looking to set goals, find balance in your life, or improve your overall well-being.

5.   **Support groups:**

- o   **Description:** These groups provide a space to share experiences, challenges and solutions with others going through similar situations.
- o **When to consult them:** If you feel the need to connect with others who understand what you are going through.

6.   **Online services and applications:**

- o **Description:** Many online platforms offer therapy, coaching and support services.
- o **When to consult them:** If you prefer a more flexible approach or if you have geographic constraints.

Bottom line:

Recognizing burnout and seeking professional help are crucial steps toward recovery. It is essential to remember that asking for help is not a sign of weakness, but rather a proactive step towards wellness and recovery. Every individual is unique, and what works for one person may not work for another. It is therefore important to find the professional or resource that best suits your specific needs.

5.2.2 Support Groups

Support groups play a vital role in the healing and recovery process for many people. They provide a safe space where individuals can share their experiences, challenges and successes with others who are going through similar situations. Here is an in-depth exploration of the importance and benefits of support groups:

1. **Nature of Support Groups:**
    o **Description:** Support groups are generally gatherings of people who share common experiences or challenges. These groups can be formal (professionally led) or informal (self-organized).
    o **Objective:** Provide a space for listening, sharing and mutual encouragement.
2. **Benefits of Support Groups:**
    o **Sense of belonging:** Knowing that you are not alone in your struggle can be extremely comforting.
    o **Sharing experiences:** Listening to others' stories can offer perspectives and solutions you hadn't considered.
    o **Reduced isolation:** Burnout can often lead to isolation. Support groups provide an opportunity to connect with others.
    o **Practical Tips:** Members can share strategies that have worked for them, offering practical solutions to common problems.
3. **Types of Support Groups:**
    o **Burnout-Specific Groups:** These groups focus specifically on burnout-related

challenges.

  o **Mental health groups:** These groups address broader topics such as depression, anxiety, and stress.

  o **Online Groups:** With modern technology, many support groups are found online, providing flexibility and accessibility.

4.	**How to find a Support Group:**

  o	**Recommendations:** Ask your doctor, therapist or counselor if they know of any local support groups.

  o	**Organizations:** Many nonprofit organizations offer support groups for various concerns.

  o	**Online search:** Platforms like Meetup or specialized forums may have lists of support groups.

5.	**Tips for Participating:**

  o	**Open-minded:** Each member has their own story. Listen with empathy and without judgment.

  o	**Active participation:** Share your experiences when you feel comfortable, but also respect your own pace.

  o **Confidentiality:** What is shared in the group must stay in the group.

Conclusion:

Support groups provide a valuable platform for healing and mutual understanding. They remind individuals that they are not alone in their struggle and provide tools and resources to navigate the recovery process. If you or someone you know is going through a difficult time, consider joining or starting a support group.

5.2.3 Applications and Digital Tools

In the age of technology, digital applications and tools play a crucial role in promoting well-being and managing burnout. These resources provide unprecedented accessibility and convenience for those looking to improve their mental health. Here is a detailed exploration of these tools:

1. **Meditation and Mindfulness Applications:**

· **Description:** These apps offer guided meditation sessions, breathing exercises, and mindfulness teachings.

· **Popular examples:** Headspace, Calm, Insight Timer.

· **Benefits:** Help reduce stress, improve concentration and promote better quality sleep.

2. **Mood Tracking Apps:**

· **Description:** Allow users to track their daily mood, identify patterns, and take proactive action.

· **Popular examples:** Daylio, Moodnotes, eMoods.

· **Benefits:** Provide awareness of one's own emotions and help identify potential triggers.

3. **Online Therapy Applications:**

· **Description:** Provide access to professional therapists via chats, video calls or messages.

· **Popular examples:** Talkspace, BetterHelp, 7 Cups.

· **Benefits:** Provide flexibility and convenience for those who may have barriers to traditional therapy.

4. Time Management and Productivity Tools:

· **Description:** Help organize tasks, prioritize responsibilities and manage time effectively.

· **Popular examples:** Todoist, Trello, Notion.

· **Benefits:** Reduce feelings of being overwhelmed and improve work efficiency.

5. Fitness and Physical Well-being Applications:

· **Description:** Offer workouts, nutritional advice and progress trackers.

· **Popular examples:** MyFitnessPal, Fitbit, Nike Training Club.

· **Benefits:** Encourage an active lifestyle, which can improve mood and reduce stress.

6. Sleep Applications:

· **Description:** Help track sleep patterns, provide soothing sounds and tips to improve sleep quality.

7. Popular examples: Sleep Cycle, Relax Melodies, Noisli.

· **Benefits:** Promote restful sleep, essential for mental and physical recovery.

Conclusion:

Digital apps and tools offer a wealth of resources

to support mental health and well-being. Whether it's for meditation, therapy or time management, there's an app to help everyone navigate the challenges of modern life and prevent or manage burnout. It is essential to choose the tools that best suit your individual needs and use them proactively.

5.2.4 Books and Publications

Books and publications are excellent resources for deepening your understanding of burnout, discovering management strategies and drawing inspiration from the experiences of others. Here is a detailed exploration of these resources:

1. **Practical Guides:**

· **Description:** These books offer practical advice, exercises and strategies for managing stress, avoiding burnout and improving overall well-being.

· **Popular examples:**

· "Burnout: The Secret to Unlocking the Stress Cycle" by Emily Nagoski and Amelia Nagoski.

· "The Joy of Burnout: How the End of the World Can Be a New Beginning" by Dina Glouberman.

· **Benefits:** They provide tangible tools and actionable steps for burnout prevention and recovery.

2. **Personal Stories:**

· **Description:** These books chronicle the authors' personal experiences with burnout, providing an intimate and real perspective.

· **Popular examples:**

· "Girl, Stop Apologizing" by Rachel Hollis.

· "Break: Harnessing the Life-Changing Power of Giving Yourself a Break" by Rachael O'Meara.

· **Benefits:** They provide a sense of camaraderie, showing that others have gone through and overcome similar challenges.

3. Research and Studies:

· **Description:** These publications focus on scientific studies, research and analysis around burnout, providing an evidence-based perspective.

· **Popular examples:**

· "Burnout for Experts: Prevention in the Context of Living and Working" edited by Sabine Bährer-Kohler.

· "The Truth About Burnout: How Organizations Cause Personal Stress and What to Do About It" by Christina Maslach.

· **Benefits:** They provide an in-depth understanding of causes, effects, and solutions based on solid research.

4. Books on Mindfulness and Meditation:

· **Description:** These books offer techniques and practices for cultivating mindfulness, an essential skill for managing stress and avoiding burnout.

· **Popular examples:**

· "Wherever You Go, There You Are" by Jon Kabat-Zinn.

· "The Miracle of Mindfulness: An Introduction to the Practice of Meditation" by Thich Nhat Hanh.

· **Benefits:** They offer techniques for staying grounded, present and aware, reducing the risk of burnout.

Conclusion:

Books and publications offer a wealth of information, advice and perspectives on burnout. From how-to guides to personal stories to in-depth research, there are a wealth of resources to help those looking to understand, prevent or recover from burnout. Choosing readings that resonate with one's own experiences and needs is essential to getting the most out of these resources.

5.2.5 Workshops and Seminars

Workshops and seminars are educational platforms that provide an opportunity for interactive learning and direct engagement with experts in the field of wellness, mental health and burnout prevention. Here is a detailed exploration of these resources:

1. **Objective of the Workshops:**

· **Description:** Workshops are typically practical sessions, focused on learning specific skills or implementing techniques to manage stress, improve well-being and prevent burnout.

· **Examples:** Stress management workshops, mindfulness workshops, breathing workshops.

· **Benefits:** They provide a hands-on learning

experience, allowing participants to practice and master techniques in real time.

2. Objective of the Seminars:

· **Description:** Seminars are often conferences or presentations given by experts, researchers or professionals in the field. They provide information, research and case studies on burnout and mental health.

· **Examples:** Conferences on the latest research on burnout, seminars on positive psychology.

· **Benefits:** They provide an educational perspective, allowing participants to gain knowledge and understand current trends.

3. Interactivity and Networking:

· **Description:** These events often provide networking opportunities, allowing participants to network with other professionals, share experiences and create connections.

· **Advantages:** They promote the creation of a community of support, essential for the prevention and recovery of burnout.

4. Additional Resources:

· **Description:** Many workshops and seminars provide additional resources, such as manuals, guides, or online tools, to help participants continue their learning after the event.

· **Benefits:** These resources reinforce learning and provide ongoing support.

· **Accessibility:**

· **Description:** With the rise of technology, many workshops and seminars are now available online, providing greater flexibility and accessibility.

· **Benefits:** This allows a wider audience to benefit from these resources, regardless of their geographic location.

Conclusion:

Workshops and seminars play a crucial role in raising awareness of burnout and providing tools and strategies to manage it. They offer a combination of theoretical and practical learning, enhanced by direct interaction with experts and a supportive community. For those looking to deepen their understanding of burnout or learn skills to manage it, these platforms are great resources to explore.

5.2.6 Wellness Retreats

Wellness retreats are organized getaways in often peaceful and natural locations, designed to offer participants a break from their daily routine and immerse them in an environment focused on health, relaxation and regeneration. Here is a detailed exploration of these retreats:

1. **Objective of Retreats:**

· **Description:** These retreats offer a combination of physical, mental and spiritual activities to revitalize the body, mind and soul.

· **Examples:** Yoga, meditation, holistic therapies, nature hikes, nutrition workshops.

· **Benefits:** They offer an immersive experience, allowing participants to disconnect from their daily stresses and reconnect with themselves.

2. Natural environment :

· **Description:** Most wellness retreats are located in natural environments, such as mountains, forests or beaches.

· **Benefits:** Nature has a calming effect on the mind and body, helping to reduce stress, improve sleep quality and increase feelings of well-being.

3. Tailor-made programs:

· **Description:** Many retreats offer personalized programs based on individual needs and preferences.

· **Benefits:** This allows for a more personal and tailored experience, maximizing benefits for each participant.

4. Professional Expertise:

· **Description:** These retreats are often led by experts in various fields of wellness.

· **Benefits:** Participants benefit from professional advice and guidance, ensuring a safe and rewarding experience.

5. Support Community:

· **Description:** Attending a retreat provides the opportunity to meet others with similar goals and aspirations.

· **Benefits:** Connecting with other participants can provide ongoing support after retirement, reinforcing commitment to a healthy lifestyle.

6. Sustainability and Eco-responsibility:

· **Description:** Many retreats adopt sustainable practices, with an emphasis on eco-responsibility.

· **Benefits:** This offers an environmentally friendly experience, aligned with the values of well-being and nature preservation.

Conclusion:

Wellness retreats are a great way to step back from everyday life, recharge and refocus. They offer a unique combination of relaxation, revitalizing activities and learning, all in a soothing natural setting. For those looking to escape the hustle and bustle of everyday life and invest in their well-being, a retreat can be a transformative experience.

5.2.7 Organizations and Associations

Organizations and associations dedicated to well-being and mental health play a crucial role in raising awareness, educating and supporting individuals with the challenges of stress, burnout and other mental health issues. Here is an in-depth exploration of these entities:

1. Main role :

· **Description:** These organizations' primary mission is to promote mental health, offer educational resources, support research, and provide direct assistance to people in need.

· **Examples:** Organizations like the WHO

(World Health Organization), the APA (American Psychological Association), or local mental health associations.

2. Awareness Programs:

· **Description:** Many organizations run awareness campaigns to educate the public about the importance of mental health and the signs of distress.

· **Benefits:** These programs help destigmatize mental health issues and encourage people to seek help.

3. Learning resources :

· **Description:** These entities often provide free or low-cost resources, such as brochures, webinars, workshops and training.

· **Benefits:** These resources allow individuals to better understand their own experiences and find coping strategies.

4. Direct Support:

· **Description:** Many organizations offer direct services such as crisis lines, support groups, therapy or referrals to professionals.

· **Benefits:** These services provide immediate and specialized support to people in distress.

5. Research and development :

· **Description:** Some associations are dedicated to mental health research, funding studies and projects to better understand and treat mental problems.

· **Advantages:** Research contributes to the evolution of treatments and the discovery of new intervention methods.

6. Collaboration and Partnerships:

· **Description:** By collaborating with other entities, governments, businesses or NGOs, these organizations can expand their reach and have a more significant impact.

· **Benefits:** These collaborations enable large-scale initiatives, reach a wider audience and mobilize more resources.

Conclusion:

Organizations and associations dedicated to mental health and well-being are essential pillars in the fight against burnout and other mental health problems. They not only provide valuable resources, but also create a community of support for those who need it. Engaging with these organizations, whether as a beneficiary or contributor, can make a significant difference in the lives of many people.

5.2.8 Employee Assistance Programs (EAP)

Employee Assistance Programs (EAPs) are services established by employers to support the mental, emotional and physical well-being of their employees. These programs offer a variety of services to help employees manage personal and professional challenges. Here is a detailed exploration of these programs:

1. Primary objective :

· **Description:** The primary purpose of EAPs is to provide confidential support to employees to help them resolve personal or professional issues that could affect their job performance.

· **Benefits:** They help improve the overall well-being of employees, reduce absenteeism and increase productivity.

2. Offered services :

· **Counseling:** EAPs often offer counseling sessions for issues such as stress, anxiety, family conflict, addiction and other mental health issues.

· **Referral:** They can refer employees to specialists or external resources for specific needs.

· **Workshops and Training:** Some EAPs offer workshops on topics such as stress management, communication, time management and other essential skills.

3. Confidentiality :

· **Description:** EAPs guarantee the confidentiality of employee information. Specific details of an employee's issues or concerns are generally not shared with the employer.

· **Benefits:** This encourages employees to use the service without fear of professional repercussions.

4. Benefits for Employers:

· **Reduced Absenteeism:** By helping employees manage personal issues, EAPs can reduce absenteeism from work.

·   **Improved Productivity:** Employees who are mentally and emotionally healthy are more likely to be productive and engaged in their work.

·   **Reduced Turnover:** Employees who feel supported are less likely to leave their jobs.

5. Access and Use:

·   **Ease of Access:** Employers generally strive to make EAPs easily accessible, whether by telephone, online or in person.

·   **Awareness:** It is essential that employees are informed of the existence of the EAP and how to access it.

Bottom Line:

Employee Assistance Programs are a valuable investment for employers because they help create a healthy and productive work environment. By offering support tailored to employee needs, EAPs play an essential role in promoting well-being at work and preventing burnout.

5.2.9 Community Initiatives

Community initiatives play a crucial role in supporting and promoting the well-being of individuals. These initiatives are often set up by local groups, non-governmental organizations or volunteers to meet specific community needs. Here is an in-depth exploration of these initiatives:

1. Primary objective :

·   **Description:** Community initiatives aim to

create a healthy and supportive environment where individuals can find support, share experiences and access resources.

· **Benefits:** They strengthen community ties, promote inclusion and offer solutions adapted to local challenges.

2. Types of Initiatives:

· **Support Groups:** These groups provide a space where individuals can share their experiences, find emotional support and get advice.

· **Workshops and Trainings:** Organized to educate community members on various topics such as stress management, mindfulness, or effective communication.

· **Awareness Events:** These events aim to inform the public about specific topics, such as preventing burnout or promoting mental well-being.

3. Participation and Commitment:

· **Volunteering:** Many individuals volunteer their time in these initiatives, offering their time and skills to support others.

· **Collaborations:** Community initiatives often collaborate with other organizations, schools or businesses to maximize their impact.

4. Resources and Funding:

· **Donations and Fundraising:** Many initiatives rely on donations from the public or organize fundraisers to finance their activities.

· **Grants:** Some initiatives may receive grants from

local governments or philanthropic organizations.

5. Impact on the Community:

· **Strengthening Ties:** These initiatives strengthen ties between community members, creating a sense of belonging.

· **Stigma Reduction:** By raising awareness and educating the public, these initiatives can help reduce the stigma associated with mental health issues.

Conclusion:

Community initiatives are essential to creating healthy and supportive environments. They provide valuable support to those who need it, while strengthening the cohesion and resilience of the community as a whole. By actively engaging in these initiatives, each individual can play a role in promoting collective well-being.

5.2.10 Educational Resources

Educational resources play a vital role in preventing, understanding and managing burnout and other mental health issues. They offer valuable information and practical tools to help individuals navigate the challenges of daily life. Here is a detailed exploration of these resources:

1. Primary objective :

· **Description:** Educational resources aim to inform, raise awareness and equip individuals to face mental health challenges.

·   **Advantages:** They provide a better understanding of problems, promote early intervention and help destigmatize mental health problems.

2. **Types of Resources:**

· **Online Courses:** Many websites and platforms offer online courses on mental health, stress management, mindfulness, etc.

· **Books and Publications:** There are a multitude of books, guides and specialist journals that address topics related to well-being and mental health.

· **Webinars and Conferences:** These live events allow attendees to interact with experts and get their questions answered.

3. **Access and Availability:**

· **Local Libraries:** Many libraries have sections dedicated to mental health and wellbeing.

· **Schools and Universities:** These institutions often offer educational resources to their students, including workshops, conferences, and consulting services.

4. **Target audience :**

· **Professionals:** Some materials are specifically designed for healthcare professionals, teachers or managers.

· **General Public:** Many resources are aimed at the general public, offering accessible and practical information.

5. **Update and Relevance:**

· **Current Research:** It is essential that educational resources are based on current research and evidence.

·   **Ratings and Reviews:** User feedback can help identify the most useful and relevant resources.

Conclusion:

Educational resources are a fundamental pillar for promoting mental health and well-being. They not only offer valuable information, but also practical tools to help individuals manage the challenges of daily life. By investing in education and awareness, we can create a more informed and empathetic society, ready to support those in need.

CONCLUSION

"Mindfulness is not a quick fix, but a solution that lasts."

Sharon Salzberg

Summary of Key Points

· **Definition of Burnout:**

· Burnout is a state of emotional, physical and mental exhaustion resulting from prolonged or chronic stress, often work-related, but can also be influenced by personal factors.

· **Causes and Symptoms:**

· The causes of burnout can be professional, personal or a combination of the two. Symptoms vary from person to person and can include physical, emotional and behavioral manifestations.

· **Global Impact:**

· Burnout has significant consequences not only for the individual, but also for organizations, economies and society as a whole. It is recognized worldwide as a major health problem.

· **Personal Testimonials:**

· The stories of people who have experienced and overcome burnout show the diversity of experiences and highlight resilience and the ability to heal.

· **Modern Healing Methods:**

· There are a variety of approaches to treating and preventing burnout, ranging from traditional therapies to holistic and alternative methods.

· **Wellbeing Trends for 2024:**

· Current wellness trends show a growing awareness of the importance of mental health and an integration of innovative practices to promote overall well-being.

· **Personalized Action Plan:**

· Creating a personalized action plan is essential to preventing and healing from burnout. This involves personal assessment, goal setting, daily planning, and incorporating stress management strategies.

· **Resources and Support:**

· There are many resources available to help people manage and overcome burnout, from mental health professionals to support groups and digital tools.

Conclusion:

Burnout is a complex issue that requires a multifaceted approach to its prevention and treatment. By understanding its causes, symptoms and available resources, as well as implementing proactive strategies, it is possible to overcome burnout and promote lasting well-being.

Encouragement and Inspiration for the Reader

Dear reader,

· **You are not alone:**

· First of all, know that you are not alone in this ordeal. Many people around the world have felt what you are feeling now and have found ways to overcome burnout. Simply recognizing that you need help is an important step toward healing.

· **Inner Strength:**

· Every individual has incredible, often unsuspected, inner strength that can be mobilized to overcome the most difficult challenges. Believe in your ability to heal, grow and thrive again.

· **Change is Possible:**

· Even though things may seem bleak now, know that change is not only possible, but likely. With the right support, resources and determination, you can regain balance and joy in your life.

· **The Beauty of Resilience:**

· Resilience is not only the ability to bounce

back from adversity, but also to grow and thrive through it. Your experience with burnout can ultimately lead you to a stronger, wiser version of yourself.

· **Every Day is a New Opportunity:**

· Every day is a chance to start again, learn from our mistakes, and make choices that bring us closer to our well-being. Embrace each day as a new opportunity for growth and healing.

· **Be Gentle with Yourself:**

· Healing is a journey, not a destination. There will be ups and downs, but it's essential to treat yourself with kindness, patience, and compassion every step of the way.

· **Community is Key:**

· Don't hesitate to seek support. Whether it's friends, family, professionals or support groups, surrounding yourself with caring people can make all the difference.

In Conclusion:

Your journey through burnout is unique, but know that you have everything you need to overcome this ordeal. Tap into your inner strength, seek support, and believe in your ability to heal. You are capable of much more than you imagine, and a bright future awaits you.

Book Glossary

· **Burnout:**

· State of physical, emotional and mental exhaustion resulting from prolonged work stress. Often characterized by a lack of motivation, decreased performance and a feeling of helplessness.

· **Well-being :**

· A state of health, happiness and prosperity, encompassing physical, mental and emotional health.

· **Cognitive-Behavioral Therapies (CBT):**

· A form of psychotherapy that aims to treat problems by changing negative thoughts and behaviors.

· **Mindfulness:**

· Practice of focusing attention on the present moment, observing without judgment.

· **Medication and Psychopharmacology:**

· Use of medications to treat psychological and emotional disorders.

· **Eco-responsibility:**

· Awareness and action in favor of environmental protection in all aspects of daily life.

· **Wellness Retreats:**

· Organized stays focused on promoting health and well-being through various activities and therapies.

· **Modern Body Practices:**

· Contemporary techniques focused on movement and body awareness to improve physical and mental health.

· **Employee Assistance Programs (EAP):**

· Services offered by employers to help employees manage and overcome personal and professional problems.

· **Emerging Technologies for Well-being:**

· New technological innovations designed to improve health and well-being.

· **Disinformation :**

· False or misleading information disseminated with the intent to deceive.

· **Resilience :**

· Ability to recover quickly from difficulties; tenacity.

· **Energy Therapies:**

· Therapeutic approaches that focus on manipulating and rebalancing the body's energy fields.

· **Expressive Therapies:**

· Use of the arts (music, dance, drawing, etc.) as a therapeutic means.

· **Functional Medicine:**

· A holistic approach to medicine that focuses on identifying and addressing the root causes of disease.

This glossary provides a brief definition of key terms used throughout the book. For a more in-depth understanding, it is recommended to refer to the relevant sections of the book.

Additional Resources

· **Websites and Applications:**

· **Mindful.org:** A complete guide to mindfulness, meditation and well-being.

· **Headspace:** Meditation and sleep app to help manage stress and anxiety.

· **Calm:** Offers guided meditations, bedtime stories, and breathing exercises.

· **Books :**

· **"The Inner Solution"** by Thierry Janssen: Explores emotional and spiritual healing.

· **"The Power of the Present Moment"** by Eckhart Tolle: Guide to living in the present and eliminating stress.

· **"Burnout: Detecting and Preventing It"** by Christina Maslach: Scientific approach to burnout and advice for preventing it.

· **Workshops and Courses:**

· **Retreat Guru:** Platform to find wellness and meditation retreats worldwide.

· **Coursera & Udemy:** Offer online courses on wellness, stress management, and mindfulness.

· **Organizations:**

· **International Association for Stress Management:** Resources and research on stress management.

· **Mindfulness Foundation:** Promote the practice

of mindfulness through educational programs.

· **Podcasts:**

· **"Le Gratin"** by Pauline Laigneau: Interviews with inspiring people about their journey and their well-being.

· **"Feel Better, Live More"** by Dr. Rangan Chatterjee: Discussions on health, wellness and productivity.

· **Videos and Documentaries:**

· **"Innsaei – The Power of Intuition"** : Documentary exploring the importance of intuition and mindfulness in the modern world.

· **TED Talks:** Talks on various topics related to well-being, mental health and productivity.

· **Online Communities:**

· **Reddit r/Mindfulness:** Forum to discuss mindfulness and share resources.

· **Well+Good:** Online community dedicated to well-being, health and fitness.

These additional resources are designed to provide ongoing support and deeper exploration of the topics covered in the book. It is recommended that you regularly consult these resources to stay informed of the latest wellness trends and research.

Sources for Writing the Book

The writing of this book was based on a combination of academic research, interviews with experts and personal testimonies. Here is a list of the main sources used:

· **Books and Publications:**

· *Burnout: The Secret to Unlocking the Stress Cycle* by Emily Nagoski and Amelia Nagoski.

· *The Telomere Effect: A Revolutionary Approach to Living Younger, Healthier, Longer* by Dr. Elizabeth Blackburn and Dr. Elissa Epel.

· *The Upside of Stress: Why Stress Is Good for You, and How to Get Good at It* by Dr. Kelly McGonigal.

· **Academic Articles:**

· Journal of Applied Psychology: "Burnout and Work Engagement: A Thorough Investigation of the Independence of Both Constructs."

· Harvard Business Review: "Beating Burnout" and "The Burnout Crisis."

· The Lancet: "Burnout in the Medical Profession: A Global Concern."

· **Websites and Blogs:**

· World Health Organization (WHO): www.who.int

· Mayo Clinic: www.mayoclinic.org

· Mindful.org: www.mindful.org

· **Interviews and Testimonials:**

· Interviews with mental health professionals, life coaches, nutritionists and wellness experts.

· Testimonials from people who have experienced and overcome burnout.

· **Reports and Studies:**

· Gallup's State of the Global Workplace Report.

· World Economic Forum's Global Competitiveness Report.

· Deloitte's Global Human Capital Trends.

· **Conferences and Workshops:**

· TED Talks on well-being, stress and burnout.

· Workshops and seminars on mindfulness, stress management and well-being at work.

· **Other Resources:**

· Wellness and meditation apps like Headspace, Calm and Insight Timer.

· Documentaries and films on well-being, stress and mental health.

It is important to note that although these sources were used to inform the writing of the book, the interpretation and presentation of the information is the author's own. It is always recommended to consult experts and professionals for personalized advice.

Questionnaires and Self-Assessments:

Here are some questionnaires and self-assessments to help you assess your stress level, your risk of burnout and your general well-being:

1. Burnout Risk Assessment

Over the past few weeks, how often have you experienced the following?

(0 = Never, 1 = Rarely, 2 = Sometimes, 3 = Often, 4 = Very often)
· Physical or mental exhaustion.
· Feeling distanced or cynical about your work.
· Feeling like you're not accomplishing much or not being effective at work.
· Difficulty concentrating or staying focused.
· Irritability or impatience with colleagues or customers.
· Using food, drugs, or alcohol to make you feel better or not to feel.
Total score: If your score is above 18, you may be at risk of burnout. Consider consulting a professional.

2. Stress Questionnaire

In the past month, how often have you been bothered by the following due to stress?
(0 = Never, 1 = Rarely, 2 = Sometimes, 3 = Often, 4 = Very often)
· Headache.
· Sleep problems.
· Feelings of depression or anxiety.
· Irritability or anger.
· Fatigue or lack of energy.
· Feeling overwhelmed or overwhelmed.
Total Score: If your score is above 18, your stress level could be cause for concern. Consider stress management techniques or consult a professional.

3. Assessment of General Well-being
Please indicate how often you experience the following:
(0 = Never, 1 = Rarely, 2 = Sometimes, 3 = Often, 4 = Very often)
· I feel healthy and full of energy.
· I am satisfied with my life.
· I feel close to others and they feel close to me.
· I managed to find a good balance between work and leisure.
· I feel capable of handling daily challenges.
· I feel motivated and inspired.
Total score: A high score indicates a high level of overall well-being. Continue to practice healthy habits and look for ways to further improve your well-being.

These questionnaires are general self-assessment tools and should not replace a professional assessment. If anyone feels concerned about their answers, they should consult a healthcare professional or counselor.

Practical exercises

1. Gratitude Journal:
Every evening, write down three things you are grateful for. This can help refocus your mind on the positive aspects of your life.
2. Deep Breathing:
Sit comfortably, close your eyes and breathe

deeply through your nose for four seconds, hold your breath for four seconds, then slowly exhale through your mouth for four seconds. Repeat this exercise for a few minutes.

3. Mindfulness Meditation:

Sit or lie down comfortably. Close your eyes and focus on your breathing. If your mind starts to wander, gently bring your attention back to your breathing.

4. Visualization Exercise:

Close your eyes and imagine a place where you feel peaceful and safe. Visualize all the details of this place and feel the positive sensations it gives you.

5. 5 Minute Break:

Every hour, take a 5 minute break to stretch, walk or simply relax. This can help reduce stress and increase your productivity.

6. Grounding Exercise:

Identify five things you can see, four that you can touch, three that you can hear, two that you can smell, and one that you can taste. This exercise can help you refocus and connect to the present moment.

7. Priority List:

Every morning, write down the three most important tasks you need to accomplish that day. Focus on these tasks before moving on to others.

8. Boundaries Exercise:

Identify one thing you can delegate or eliminate from your to-do list. Learning to say no or ask for help can reduce stress.

9. Practice Self-Compassion:

Take a moment to talk to yourself as you would a dear friend. Recognizing your efforts and reminding yourself that you are doing your best can help alleviate feelings of inadequacy.

10. Detachment Exercise:

Identify a stressful situation in your life. Imagine that you are looking at it from the outside, as a neutral spectator. This can help you see the situation from a different perspective and reduce your emotional reaction.

11. Reflection Journal:

At the end of each week, take a moment to reflect on what went well, what you learned, and what you would like to improve on in the following week.

12. Connection Exercise:

Spend quality time with a loved one, whether in person, on the phone, or on video. Human connection can be a powerful antidote to stress.

13. Enjoy Nature:

Spend at least 20 minutes a day outside, whether for a walk, gardening, or just sitting and enjoying nature. Connecting with nature has been shown to reduce stress and improve well-being.

14. Affirmation Exercise:

Write three positive affirmations about yourself and repeat them every morning. This can help boost your self-esteem and combat negative thoughts.

15. Disconnect Exercise:

Choose a time each day to turn off all your electronic devices and disconnect. Use this time to read, meditate, exercise, or any other activity that relaxes you.

Guide to Applications and Tools:

1. Meditation Applications:

· **Headspace:** A guided meditation app that offers short sessions for different needs, like stress, sleep, or focus.

· **Calm:** Offers meditations, bedtime stories, and breathing exercises to help reduce stress.

2. Time Management Applications:

· **Toggl:** A time tracking tool that helps you understand how you use your time each day.

· **Forest:** An app that encourages you not to use your phone for a set period of time by growing a virtual tree.

3. Sleep Tracking Apps:

· **Sleep Cycle:** Analyzes your sleep quality and wakes you during your lightest sleep phase.

· **Relax Melodies:** Offers sounds and melodies to help you fall asleep.

4. Fitness Apps:

· **MyFitnessPal:** A diet and exercise tracker to help maintain a healthy lifestyle.

· **7 Minute Workout:** Offers short workouts for those short on time.

5. Journaling Applications:

- **Day One:** A digital journal that allows you to record your thoughts, photos and places.
- **Five Minute Journal:** Encourages daily reflection with prompts for gratitude and self-reflection.

6. Mindfulness Applications:

- **Smiling Mind:** Offers mindfulness programs for all ages.
- **Insight Timer:** Offers a variety of guided meditations and music for relaxation.

7. Digital Disconnect Tools:

- **StayFocusd:** A browser extension that limits time spent on distracting sites.
- **Freedom:** Blocks access to distracting apps or websites for a set period of time.

8. Mental Health Support Apps:

- **Talkspace:** Connects users with licensed therapists for online therapy sessions.
- **BetterHelp:** Offers online counseling with mental health professionals.

9. Stress Management Applications:

- **Breathe2Relax:** Guides users through breathing exercises to reduce stress.
- **Stress & Anxiety Companion:** Provides tools for managing stress and anxiety.

Activities Calendar:

Week 1: Introduction to mindfulness
- **Monday :**

· Morning: 10-minute guided meditation to start the day.

· Evening: Journaling 5 things you are grateful for.

· **Tuesday** :

· Morning: Deep breathing exercise for 5 minutes.

· Evening: Reading a chapter on mindfulness.

· **Wednesday** :

· Morning: Mindful walk for 15 minutes.

· Evening: Gentle yoga practice for 20 minutes.

· **THURSDAY** :

· Morning: 10-minute gratitude meditation.

· Evening: Listen to a podcast on the benefits of mindfulness.

· **Friday** :

· Morning: Visualization exercise for 10 minutes.

· Evening: Free time for personal reflection.

· **Weekend** :

· Half-day mindfulness workshop.

Week 2: Stress management

· **Monday** :

· Morning: 10-minute relaxation meditation.

· Evening: Hot bath with relaxing essential oils.

· **Tuesday** :

· Morning: Stretching exercises to release tension.

· Evening: Journaling thoughts and feelings.

· **Wednesday** :

· Morning: Walk outdoors to connect with nature.

· Evening: Listening to soothing music.

- **THURSDAY :**
- Morning: Gratitude practice.
- Evening: Painting or art therapy workshop.
- **Friday :**
- Morning: Guided meditation on stress management.
- Evening: Relaxing movie night at home.
- **Weekend :**
- Workshop on relaxation techniques.

Week 3: Social Connection

- **Monday :**
- Morning: Video call with a friend or family member.
- Evening: Participation in an online support group.
- **Tuesday :**
- Morning: Sending postcards or letters to loved ones.
- Evening: Virtual dinner with friends.
- **Wednesday :**
- Morning: Participation in an online group course.
- Evening: Family board game.
- **THURSDAY :**
- Morning: Online group meditation.
- Evening: Virtual quiz night with friends.
- **Friday :**
- Morning: Sharing an inspiring quote on social media.

· Evening: Watching a film or series with a friend remotely.

· **Weekend :**

· Participation in a virtual community event.

This schedule is designed to provide structure and varied activities to improve well-being over a three-week period. It can be adapted according to individual needs and preferences.

THANKS

Writing this book has been a journey in itself, and as with any journey, there have been many fellow travelers who have made this adventure possible. It is time to express my deep gratitude to them.

First of all, I would like to thank my family for their unwavering support. To my parents, for instilling in me a love of reading and writing, and for always believing in me, even when I doubted it. To my son for being my daily source of inspiration.

I am also indebted to all my mentors, professors and colleagues who have guided me throughout my career. Your wisdom, advice, and constructive criticism have shaped this work in immeasurable ways.

Special thanks to Sophie Smith, life coach and mindfulness expert, for her enlightening foreword and for sharing her valuable knowledge with me throughout this process.

I also want to express my gratitude to everyone who shared their personal stories of burnout and recovery. Your stories brought this book to life and showed many readers that they are not alone in their fight.

Many thanks to my editor and the entire editorial team for their dedication, expertise and passion for this project. Your support has been essential in turning this vision into reality.

Finally, I would like to thank each reader who took the time to delve into these pages. It is for you that I wrote this book, in the hope that it can bring you some light, understanding and hope.

With all my gratitude,
Vincent Lefebvre